I.O. Evans Studies
in the Philosophy and Criticism of Literature
ISSN 0271-9061
Number Nineteen

DISCOVERING
Dean Koontz

*Essays on America's Bestselling Writer
of Suspense and Horror Fiction*

*Second Edition
Revised and Expanded*

Edited

by

Bill Munster

BORGO PRESS / WILDSIDE PRESS

www.wildsidepress.com

Library of Congress Cataloging-in-Publication Data

Discovering Dean Koontz : essays on America's bestselling writer of suspense and horror fiction / edited by Bill Munster. — 2nd ed., rev. and expanded.

   p. cm. — (I.O. Evans studies in the philosophy and criticism of literature, ISSN 0271-9061 ; no. 19)

   Rev. ed. of: Sudden fear. 1988.

   "A Thaddeus Dikty Book."

   Includes bibliographical references (p.) and index.

   ISBN 1-55742-144-7 (cloth). — ISBN 1-55742-145-5 (pbk.)

   1. Koontz, Dean R. (Dean Ray), 1945- —Criticism and interpretation. 2. Horror tales, American—History and criticism. I. Munster, Bill, 1947- . II. Sudden fear. III. Series: I.O. Evans studies in the philosophy & criticism of literature ; no. 19.

PS3561.O55Z88 1998   95-5206
813'.54—dc20   CIP

SECOND EDITION

CONTENTS

INTRODUCTION

You drive up out of the smoggy well of the city to visit Dean and Gerda Koontz, over a hill that'll have you downshifting a gear or two, and, if your car is as old as mine, wondering about your radiator hoses; and then when you pass the crest you're in the midst of horse trails and split-rail fences and elegant houses perched on green slopes. The Koontz house is down a lane and around a corner, far enough away from the main road so that all you hear when you get out of your car is the wind in the aromatic trees.

I'm always a little intimidated by elegance, and the first few times I visited the Koontzes I was afraid I'd leave grime on the couches—and once, when a table-full of hors d'oeuvre included a ripe German cheese, I thought, to my horror, that my shoes had begun to actively decay—but Dean is so good-natured and unassuming that guests can't help but relax. After all, the man likes to have people in ape suits appear at his parties to recite funny verses—this is not strict formality.

Soon you fall in with it. Jim Blaylock often finds it a good idea to bring over big-eyed rubber squids to set in unlikely places throughout the house—though too often Dean and Gerda fail to notice them, and Blaylock has to make do with just imagining the eventual responses—and a fairly reserved and businesslike New York editor visited the Koontzes, and in no time was enlisting my wife's help in a plan to cover the landscaped front yard with lawn flamingoes and ceramic gnomes. Dean relished this stuff—one night after a late-breaking-up party at a convention in Tucson, Dean called my wife's and my room and made menacing pig-sounds...and then stayed up for at least an hour waiting for whatever our retaliation might consist of.

You might almost begin to think of him as a sort of bookish Bertie Wooster, a man of leisure with the means to indulge a writing hobby...but by this time you've gotten to know him. You've learned that he struggled up out of an appalling, poverty-choked childhood, that he's seen a good deal of real violence, that he has written dozens and dozens of novels, under pseudonyms as well as his own name, and that until recently he was at work at his typewriter for well over ten hours every day, seven days every week. When he was racing against the deadline for delivery of his book *Whispers*, in fact, he slept four nights a week and worked straight through the other three.

Awed by this—in fact, intimidated again—your first thought is that the book can't have been good, not *really good*, if he wrote it that way. Then you read it, and when you've finished you don't even need to be told that it went through more than thirty drafts—you know already that every bit of polishing required for perfection has been done here.

And he's gotten better since. I'm confident that *Watchers* will be in print for as long as there are publishers.

These days, of course, Dean's taking it easy. He and Gerda actually went on a vacation last year, and he's taking a day a week off now, and even hopes soon to be able to take *two* days a week off. It's a big self-indulgence, and I can't imagine him ever unbending much more than that. Discipline was the lifeline by which he pulled himself up out of the narrow predestination of small-town poverty, and I'm afraid his hands have been clenched on it too long now for him ever to let go.

Speaking as a reader, that sounds fine to me; I love his books, and would like to see dozens more. But—just selfishly, speaking as a friend—I do wish he'd allow himself more time to sit around with beer in jovial company.

—Tim Powers
La Mirada, California

FOREWORD

BY BILL MUNSTER

I first met Dean Koontz in Woodstock, New York. I was out doing some last-minute Christmas shopping when I decided to see what new books had arrived at the Golden Notebook on Tinker Street.

The Golden Notebook is situated right along the main road of Woodstock. In case you're wondering, this is the same Woodstock that most people think the festival took place in back in 1969. Actually, the concert was in White Lake. Woodstock, at any time of the year, is charming. Just as important, there's no telling whom one might find walking about the streets. Remember, it's in Woodstock that people like Bob Dylan, Joan Baez, and other folk singers would lay their roots. A bit down the road from the Golden Notebook is the Bear Cafe, owned by the late Albert Grossman, who was manager for many of these folk singers, including Peter, Paul, and Mary. In addition, Lee Marvin once resided in Woodstock, as does the writer of adolescent novels, Paula Danziger.

And so it came as no surprise that I should happen to meet Dean Koontz while shopping for a last minute Christmas gift. Acutally, it wasn't Koontz in the flesh that I met, but Koontz on paper. His novel, *Phantoms*, was displayed rather prominently in a bin at the very front of the store. It looked inviting. Black cover with *Phantoms* scrawled across the front. The cover blurb, "A novel of unnatural terror by the author of the million copy bestseller *Whispers*," also sounded interesting. I turned to my wife, Marie, and said, "Looks good."

"Well, then, why don't you buy it?" she said and continued looking about the store.

But the strange thing is...I didn't buy it. Marie did. After exchanging our presents on Christmas morning, Marie suddenly handed me one more. A copy of *Phantoms*.

Now, for some inexplicable reason, that book sat unread for almost a year. It wasn't until the following winter, early November, that I sat down one weekend and read the book. Then I wanted more and read *Whispers*.

It was after reading *Whispers* that I decided that I had to interview Dean Koontz for my magazine *Footsteps VI*. I sat down and wrote a letter to Berkley:

To Whom It May Concern:

I publish a small press magazine called Footsteps. *Each issue contains material related to the horror theme—short stories, reviews, interviews, etc. For an upcoming issue, I would like to interview Dean R. Koontz by mail. Would you please advise me on how I might contact Mr. Koontz. In addition, if you have any camera-ready ads for* Phantoms, *a book I plan to discuss in the next issue of* Footsteps, *would you please send me one. In fact, any press information you have on Koontz would be greatly appreciated.*
Thank you for your time.

Sincerely yours,

Bill Munster

My letter went out, and on December 16, 1984, Dean called me on the telephone. Although we never met, we talked for close to an hour. In closing, Dean said he'd be more than happy to be interviewed for *Footsteps VI*.

What was it about *Phantoms* that grabbed me? I was struck by the craftsmanship that Koontz displayed in the telling of a story of a small town, Snowfield, California, that's nearly snuffed by a malevolent phantom. For one thing, I like stories that are set in small towns. For another, I liked the idea that the story had so much dialogue. Further, I found Koontz's small town to be much the same as Joni Mitchell's "Morning Morgantown," Paul Simon's "My Little Town," and even Bruce Springsteen's "My Hometown." Koontz shows a small town that's serene and protecting, mediocre and ordinary, and a harborer of possible violence.

And then there was *Whispers*.

Whispers, I would later learn, has over three million copies in print worldwide. I would also learn that major publishers are not without fault. As Dean would tell me in a letter dated December 23, 1984: "John D. MacDonald's name [in the inside author endorsement] is spelled wrong! I've been trying to get Berkley to correct this through 11 printings, without success." In that same letter I would learn from Dean that he would write *Whispers*, "in a white-hot fury, six months from start to finish." He would also be an emotional and physical wreck after that pace, and also because of the subject matter—Dean

Koontz had been an abused child. In addition, Koontz would touch on themes in *Whispers* that would squarely place the novel into the mainstream. Though not a horror story, the novel could be called a horrifying story of child abuse. It was also a novel that would show the effects of misguided parents. And it was a novel that would study the nature of betrayal. Hilary by her parents, Joshua by his clients, a sheriff by his deputy, and Bruno by his doctor.

What follows will be both a gentle and scholarly look at Dean Koontz's horror and dark suspense fiction. In no way is this book an attempt to study his science fiction; to do so would require the page depth of a Manhattan phone directory. Here one will find a look at *Watchers* and *Shadowfires*, by Stan Brooks; a comparative essay on the writing styles of Dean Koontz and Stephen King, by Michael R. Collings; a deeper look at *Twilight Eyes*, also by Michael Collings; an enormous study of the monsters in Koontz fiction, by Michael A. Morrison; the mainstream fiction of Dean Koontz, by D. W. Taylor; the evolution of a writer, by Stan Brooks; the powers of Koontz's words, by Richard Laymon; a look at the woman protagonist, by Elizabeth Massie; a chronology and an interview, plus an introduction by Tim Powers and an afterword by Joe Lansdale.

A book of this nature sails on rough waters with some readers. It is the understanding of some that a writer's words should speak for themselves and not require explanation by critics. True, to a point. But what we have here is a greater understanding of how Dean Koontz puts together a work of art. It's his building of words and ideas that give his books such mass appeal. It's his looking at the tenuous nature of life and the tissue-thin barrier that separates us from sudden terror and tragedy that gives his books such power and enjoyment.

Read on and see if you don't agree.

—Bill Munster
Round Top, New York

A DEAN KOONTZ CHRONOLOGY

1945 Dean Ray Koontz is born to Raymond and Florence (Logue) Koontz in Everett, Pennsylvania, as their only child.

1962 Meets Gerda Cerra at Bedford High School, Bedford, PA.

1965 (through 1966) Short story editor for the college literary magazine, *The Reflector* (Shippensburg State College, PA). Marries Gerda Cerra. Wins *Atlantic Monthly* creative writing certificate for his short story, "The Kittens."

1966 (through 1967) Teacher-Counselor with Appalachian Poverty Program; Publishes "Soft Come the Dragons" and "To Behold the Sun" (*Fantasy & Science Fiction*).

1967 (through 1969) High school English teacher in Harrisburg, PA.

1968 Publishes *Star Quest* (Ace Books); "A Darkness in My Soul" (*Fantastic Stories*); "The Psychedelic Children" and "Twelfth Bed" (*Fantasy & Science Fiction*; "Dreambird" (*Worlds of If*).

1969 After selling twenty short stories and three novels, leaves teaching to write full-time. Publishes *The Fall of the Dream Machine* (Ace); *Fear That Man* (Ace); "Temple of Sorrow" (*Amazing Stories*); "Muse" (*Fantasy & Science Fiction*); "Killerbot" (*Galaxy*); "In the Shield" and "Where the Beast Runs" (*Worlds of If*); "Dragon in the Land" (*Venture*); "Diligently Corrupting Young Minds" (*Science Fiction Review*). Declares: "I become a full-fledged writer."

1970 Publishes *Anti-Man* (Paperback); *Beastchild* (Lancer); *Dark of the Woods* (Ace); *The Dark Symphony* (Lancer); *Hell's Gate* (Lancer); "The Good Ship Lookoutworld" and "The Crimson Witch" (*Fantastic Stories*); "A Third Hand" and "The Mystery of his Flesh" (*Fantasy & Science Fiction*); "Shambolain" (*Worlds of If*); "Unseen Warriors" (*Worlds of Tomorrow*); "Nightmare Gang" (*Infinity One*, edited by Robert Hoskins, Lancer Books); *Bounce Girl* (Cameo Classics).

1971　Publishes *The Crimson Witch* (Curtis); Hugo Award nomination at the World Science Fiction Convention, for novella "Beastchild"; *Legacy of Terror* (as "Deanna Dwyer," Lancer).

1972　Publishes *A Darkness in My Soul* (DAW); *The Flesh in the Furnace* (Bantam); *Starblood* (Lancer); *Time Thieves* (Ace); *Warlock* (Lancer); *Chase* (as "K. R. Dwyer," Random House); departs from science fiction and enters the genre of suspense with *Chase*; "Altarboy" (*Infinity Three*, Lancer Books, edited by Robert Hoskins); "Ollie's Hands" (*Infinity Four*, Lancer Books, edited by Robert Hoskins); "A Mouse in the Walls of the Global Village" (*Again, Dangerous Visions*, Doubleday, edited by Harlan Ellison); *Writing Popular Fiction* (Writer's Digest).

1973　Publishes *A Werewolf Among Us* (Ballantine); *The Haunted Earth* (Lancer); *Demon Seed* (Bantam); *Shattered* (as "K. R. Dwyer," Random); *Blood Risk* (as "Brian Coffey," Bobbs-Merrill); first comic novel, *Hanging On* (M. Evans); "Terra Phobia" (*Androids, Time Machines and Blue Giraffes*, Follett, edited by Roger Elwood and Vic Ghidalia); "Wake Up to Thunder" (*Children of Infinity*, Franklin Watts, edited by Roger Elwood); "The Undercity" (*Future City*, Trident, edited by Roger Elwood); "The Sinless Child" (*Flame Tree Planet*, Concordia, edited by Roger Elwood); "Grayworld" (*Infinity Five*, Lancer, edited by Robert Hoskins).

1974　Publishes *After the Last Race* (Atheneum); *Strike Deep* (as "Anthony North," Dial); *Surrounded* (as "Brian Coffey," Bobbs-Merrill); "The Night of the Storm" (*Continuum 1*, Franklin Watts, edited by Roger Elwood); "We Three" (*Final Stage: The Ultimate Science Fiction Anthology*, Charterhouse, edited by Edward L. Ferman and Barry N. Malzberg).

1975　Publishes *The Long Sleep* (as "John Hill"): *Nightmare Journey* (Putnam); *Dragonfly* (as "K. R. Dwyer," Random); *The Wall of Masks* (as "Brian Coffey," Bobbs-Merrill); *Invasion* (as "Aaron Wolfe").

1976　Publishes *Night Chills* (Atheneum); *Prison of Ice* (as "David Axton," Lippincott).

1977　Publishes *The Vision* (Putnam); *The Face of Fear* (as "Brian Coffey," Bobbs-Merrill); *Shattered* filmed by Warner Brothers; *Demon Seed* (MGM) starring Fritz Weaver and Julie Christie.

1978   Writes for TV show, *CHiPs* (as "Brian Coffey").

1979   Publishes *The Key to Midnight* (as "Leigh Nichols," Pocket).

1980   Publishes *Whispers* (Putnam); *The Funhouse* (as "Owen West," Jove).

1981   Publishes *The Mask* (as "Owen West," Jove); *The Eyes of Darkness* (as "Leigh Nichols," Pocket); *The Voice of the Night* (as "Brian Coffey," Doubleday); *How to Write Best-Selling Fiction* (Writer's Digest); *Heartbeeps: A Novel* (as "John Hill," Jove).

1982   Publishes *The House of Thunder* (as "Leigh Nichols," Pocket).

1983   Publishes *Phantoms* (Putnam).

1984   Publishes *Darkfall* (Berkley); *Twilight* (as "Leigh Nichols," Pocket).

1985   Enters the speciality press field with a 120,000 word, illustrated novel, *Twilight Eyes* (Land of Enchantment); publishes *The Door to December* (as "Richard Paige," NAL).

1986   Founding President of The Horror Writers of America; publishes two short stories, "Down in the Darkness," and "Weird World" in *The Horror Show*; short story, "The Black Pumpkin" and interview by Joe Lansdale appear in the December *Twilight Zone*; the short story "Snatchers" and interview with Bill Munster appear in the fall *Night Cry*; *Strangers* (Putnam).

1987   Film rights to *Watchers* sold to Roger Corman's Concorde Pictures.   Publishes short story "The Interrogation" appears in *The Horror Show* (Fall); *Watchers* (Putnam); *Shadowfires* (as "Leigh Nichols," Avon); expanded *Twilight Eyes* (W. H. Allen in UK, Berkley in US); "Keeping the Reader on the Edge of His Seat" (*How to Write Tales of Horror, Fantasy, and Science Fiction*, Writer's Digest); "The Coming Blaylocian Age" (*Two Views of a Cave Painting*, Axolotl). *Strangers* is a finalist for the World Fantasy Award.

1988   Publishes short stories "Miss Attila the Hun," "Twilight of the Dawn," and "Hardshell" in *Night Visions 4* (Dark Harvest); *Lightning* (Putnam). *Lightning* (Simon and Schuster Audioworks); "Graveyard Highway" (*Tropical Chills*, Avon); *Oddkins: A Fable for All Ages* (Warner Books). Appears as a special guest on *Hour 25* (KPFK-FM) in Los Angeles, CA on

January 15, 1988. The film *Watchers* (Concorde Films), starring Corey Haim and Barbara Williams, is released. *Sudden
Fear: The Horror and Dark Suspense Fiction of Dean R.
Koontz,* edited by Bill Munster, the first critical guide to the
works of Dean Koontz, is published by Starmont House. *The
Servants of Twilight* (originally published as *Twilight*), is produced in a limited hardcover edition (Dark Harvest).

1989   Publishes *Midnight* (Putnam); *Midnight* (Brill).   Writes the
        screenplay for *Darkfall* (Warner Bros.).   Paramount purchases
        film rights to *Midnight*.   *The Key to Midnight* appears in a
        limited hardcover edition (Dark Harvest).   "Trapped" appears
        in *Stalkers* (Dark Harvest, ed. by Martin H. Greenberg and Ed
        Gorman).

1990   Publishes *The Bad Place* (Putnam); *Servants of Twilight*
        (Berkley).   Writes unproduced *Night Chills* teleplay (by
        "Robert Crais").   Writes *The Bad Place* (unproduced screen-
        play for Warner Bros.); *Midnight* (screenplay for Warner
        Bros.) *The Face of Fear* (teleplay, CBS-TV, Sept. 30, 1990).
        The film *Whispers* (Cinepix) is released, starring Victoria Ten-
        nant.

1991   Publishes *Cold Fire* (Putnam); *Three Complete Novels* (Wings
        Books).

1992   Publishes *Hideaway* (Putnam).

1993   Publishes *Mr. Murder* (Putnam); *Dragon Tears* (Putnam);
        Trapped (Eclipse Graphic Novels), illustrated by Anthony Bi-
        lau, adapted by Ed Gorman; *Mr. Murder* (Simon and Schuster
        Audioworks); *Dragon Tears* (Simon and Schuster Au-
        dioworks).

1994   Publishes *Winter Moon* (Ballantine); *Dark Rivers of the Heart*
        (Charnel House).   The film *Hideaway* (Tristar) is released,
        starring Jeff Goldblum and Alicia Silverstone.   *The Dean
        Koontz Companion,* edited by Bill Munster, Martin Green-
        berg, and Ed Gorman (Headline and Berkley).

1995   Publishes *Strange Highways* (Warner Books); *Icebound*
        (Ballantine); *Icebound* (Random House Audiobooks); *Chase*
        (Time-Warner Audiobooks); *Strange Highways* (Time-Warner
        Audiobooks).

1996 Publishes *Intensity* (Knopf); *Santa's Twin* (HarperPrism); *Beautiful Death: Art of the Cemetery*, photographs by David Robinson (Penguin Studio). *Dean Koontz: A Critical Companion*, by Joan G. Kotker, is published by Greenwood Press.

1997 Publishes *Sole Survivor* (Knopf). *Dean Koontz: A Writer's Biography*, by Katherine M. Ramsland, is published by HarperPrism.

1998 Publishes *Fear Nothing* (Bantam) and *Three Novels* (Putnam).

I.

MIDNIGHT:

ANATOMY OF A THRILLER

BY BILL MUNSTER

"Though this be madness, yet there is method in't."
—William Shakespeare

The academic in me thought it would be interesting to take a careful look at one of Dean Koontz's novels to see how he composes a story. Though he says he hasn't formally outlined a novel since *Phantoms*, there are certain integral parts of his stories that make them worthy of exploring how Koontz successfully executes a novel, first in his head, then on paper, where the well-developed characters carry off the tale.

Midnight presents a narrative structure overwhelmingly complex in design, but quite lucid to follow. It is a collage of characters, events, ideas, and setting which, through careful manipulation by the author, becomes an engaging techno-thriller. It is, in my opinion, one of Koontz's best works.

What follows will be an exploration of how each part of *Midnight* contributes to the whole of the novel. We will see how events are connected and not randomly tossed in, this despite the absence of outlining by Koontz. By carefully examining the novel, we can see clearly how passages in a given section all contribute to the outcome of the novel. By looking at the structure of *Midnight*, we can see the intricate development of exposition, complication, and finally, resolution. These clever layerings of moments are what gives *Midnight* its narrative momentum.

PART ONE

ALONG THE NIGHT COAST

*"Where eerie figures caper
to some midnight music
that only they can hear. "*
—*The Book of Counted Sorrows*

The trademark of a Koontz novel is a quote from that mythical collection, *The Book of Counted Sorrows*. Beginning a novel with an epigram sets the reader's mind in the right direction. Given the diverse story ideas of Koontz's works, and its multiple themes, it is not always easy fo find a suitable quote to begin his stories. Hence, Koontz has created in his own (and in the reader's mind) a single book that he frequently taps for quotes, and which many a fan has mistaken for real.

CHAPTER 1

The novel begins with a calculated risk: a minor character, Janice Capshaw, who will prove later in the novel to be very important, is murdered while jogging along a tranquil beach. We are told just enough about Capshaw to feel empathy for her death—she was well liked in town, and her husband, Richard, a Lutheran minister, had recently succumbed to cancer. On the one hand, beginning a novel with a murder seems almost sensational, but as one reads on, we see that this was the most logical way to start. It is this murder that will bring two other major characters to Moonlight Cove to unravel a chain of bizarre happenings. Furthermore, this opening chapter plunges the reader immediately into the novel. Suspicions are introduced. Curiosity is aroused. There is a tiny glimpse of Moonlight Cove as Koontz brushes on scenes of impressionist imagery. Finally, there is no narrative padding to make the reader feel cheated.

CHAPTER 2

As stated in the novel, "On Monday, October 13, twenty-two days after the death of Janice Capshaw, Sam Booker drove his rental car from the San Francisco International Airport to Moonlight Cove." Sam, as we will soon learn, is an FBI agent sent to investigate the murders that have been happening. For Sam, a major character, and perhaps Koontz's most colorful one, life can be summed up in four ways: a cold glass of Guinness Stout, Mexican food, his love for Goldie Hawn, and the fear of death. Make no mistake about it, Sam is your everyman. This chapter is more than just an opportunity to introduce a major character, it is a way of underscoring the fact that things are not right in Moonlight Cove. Through Sam's eyes, we are told that the town possesses a "powerful strangeness." Even a gentle fog will take on a menacing stance as its "serpentine tendrils" rise off the choppy ocean.

CHAPTER 3

The next major character is introduced: Chrissie Foster, an eleven-year-old girl who is running from something. Chrissie, we soon learn, has been hiding from her parents, Alex and Sharon, in the pantry. Why? It is critical to the understanding of this character that we recognize that she is an intelligent young lady, whose imagination has been fired by reading some of the most popular adolescent novelists—Paul Zindel, Daniel Manus Pinkwater, and Andre Norton. This is not just a dropping of names, because it shows why Chrissie, who wants to be a writer when she grows up, relies heavily upon her imagination in creating a situation that her favorite writer would concoct to deal with reality. It's this creative thinking that keeps Chrissie alive. When she hits upon a clever idea to use an aerosol spray-gun as a means of defense, her mind quickly leaps into a tabloid headline set of gears: "Ingenious Young Girl Saves Self with Ordinary Household Lubricant." Chrissie, it seems, has no fear of death. There is also a sense of irony in this chapter when Chrissie begins to think about Robert Louis Stevenson's *The Strange Case of Dr. Jekyll and Mr. Hyde* during a tense moment. Clearly, Koontz is having a good time playing literary table tennis with the great writers of our time.

CHAPTER 4

The action returns to Sam as he steps inside the Knight's Bridge Tavern for a drink. Through a congenial conversation with the bar's owner, Burr Peckham, Sam reveals his reasons for being in Moonlight Cove. The reader, who will only learn the truth later in the novel, is told that Sam is a retired stock broker who made it big in the stock market and is now looking for a place to settle down. This chapter also gives us another glimpse into the town itself. We are told that an overwhelming feeling of solitude hangs over the town. The bar itself enhances the notion that Moonlight Cove is a place of death and sorrow. Once again, nature, in the form of a lingering fog, will give the impression that the town is vacant. This ominous state of nature has a powerful hold on Sam. For Sam, the night and fog provide him with a sense of curiosity, power, and even inspiration. More importantly, this chapter sends Sam to Cove Lodge on Cypress Lane to stay for awhile. It is here that fate will play an important part in the novel.

CHAPTER 5

Chrissie Foster has managed to bolt from her home and into the safety of the night fog. This same fog that gave Sam feelings of unease provides Chrissie with a sense of comfort. Quickly, she races to her barn and to the stall of her horse, Godiva, to ride to safety. Contrast plays an important part here. In the preceding chapter, we saw Sam casually drinking a beer and preparing to stay in a local motel. Playing against that is a young girl running for her life. Just as important, we are shown the elements (regressives) that are chasing the young girl through the woods. If ever there were a character in the pit of isolation and terror, it is Chrissie.

CHAPTER 6

Sam Booker has checked into the Cove Lodge and is now warm and safe in his room. His story of being retired, we now learn, was a cover to his true identity of an undercover law enforcement agent. In addition, we learn that Sam hates undercover work. It is also in this chapter that we learn that Sam's wife, Karen, is dead, and that they have a son, Scott. The relationship between Sam and Scott is not the best. In only a few short chapters, Koontz has given enough information about two central characters, Chrissie Foster and Sam Booker, to make us concerned about their situation.

CHAPTER 7

While Sam is preparing to leave for dinner, Tessa June Lockland, the sister of Janice Capshaw, has checked into the Cove Lodge. Tessa is a tough individual who, like her murdered sister, Janice Capshaw, will not be found in any corner "feeling sorry for herself." Though this is a short chapter, it tells us enough about Tessa to make the reader see that she does not accept the stories that the officials have told her about the death of her sister. She needs to find out for herself what really happened. Moreover, Tessa is convinced that if she can go down to the beach where her sister was killed, she will gain some sense of insight or the "flicker of intuition" into the real reason for the death of her sister. Again, we have a stark contrast in characters. Where Sam can only see the loneliness and despair of Moonlight Cove, Tessa sees reasons to find out what is going on.

CHAPTER 8

Chrissie Foster continues to run and hide. Not only is the situation of having an evil entity chasing her through the dark woods troubling Chrissie, so too is nature itself becoming a malevolent creature. A

18

portrait of night terrors is painted: "...the hammered-silver moon rose about the dark eastern hills...." Later, the leaves, "a scarlet blaze of autumn color in daylight but now as black as bits of funeral shrouds," will haunt the young girl. Through simple but well-considered language, Koontz presents striking details. The scene is eerie, enhancing the confusion and menace surrounding Chrissie. Again, to pull her though this nightmare world, Chrissie runs imaginary lines of fiction through her mind. As the chapter ends, Koontz drops a simple, but shocking three-word sentence when Chrissie peers out of her hiding place at the creatures, and asks, "What are you?"

CHAPTER 9

A writer can reveal character in five ways: what a character says, the way a character behaves, the thoughts that run through a character's mind, the outward appearance of a character, and what other people say. Koontz taps all of these methods to reveal his characters. It is also interesting to note that with Koontz we immediately know a character. He quickly has the reader become involved with each character he introduces. There is an inner feeling that we have met these people before in some walk of life. Tessa Lockland is one of those characters. She is a self-assured (much like the younger Chrissie), and has a clear sense of what she wants to accomplish in Moonlight Cove: find out the truth of her sister's death. Her profession, that of a "film-maker specializing in industrials and documentaries of various kinds," lends itself to her characterization. By being a film-maker of documentaries, she tends to see the world as it really is and not as it could or should be, as would someone making films based on fiction. Her observations are keen, with a close attention to detail. In her chosen field, she immerses herself in the subject of a documentary and then films it, absorbing, if you will, the soul of her subject. To date, Tessa has not failed anyone. As we will learn later in the book, she is a highly responsible individual and will often teach these values to others. In short, she is hell-bent on finding out the real reason for her sister's death. On that notion, she goes to the beach where her sister died to see if she can gain some understanding and insight into what really happened. With all her self-assurance, Tessa still feels a sense of dread as she leaves the beach to return to her hotel.

CHAPTER 10

Thomas Shaddock floats in his sensory-deprivation chamber. This Ichabod Crane of a character is so aroused by this lonely chamber that he becomes erect and sexually stimulated by the warm fluid that keeps him afloat, as well as by his dreams of power. When he reaches orgasm, "milky threads of semen" fill the chamber's magnesium-sulfate solution. This arabesque description of Shaddock, coupled with his sexual gratification in the chamber, introduces a person of evil vitality.

CHAPTER 11

While Shaddock lies safely in his chamber, Chrissie continues her flight from the dark creatures of the night. In direct contrast (a literary key to the development of these opening chapters) to Shaddock's chamber, Chrissie finds peace, if you will, while hiding in a pipe that is four feet in diameter. Just as Shaddocks's senses are charged, so too are Chrissie's to the things that roam the woods in search of her. Like an embryo, Chrissie will lie in wait in the culvert until it's safe to come out.

CHAPTER 12

Up to this point, the emphasis of the novel has been on introducing the major characters. Now it's time to reveal plot in greater depth. Sam Booker is sitting in the Perez Family Restaurant. The reader knows that at some level Sam is suspicious and not totally sure of what is going on in Moonlight Cove. We know, too, that there have not been that many people along the streets of this California town. Here, however, in the warm restaurant, is a fairly large crowd of people eating. Yet, despite their numbers, the restaurant itself is uncannily quiet. Hints are dropped in the narrative that things are clearly not right. People eat with enormous force. There is almost a fevered pitch to the way the patrons devour their meals. Furthermore, the diners are either drinking milk, ice water, or Cokes. This, we soon learn, explains the lack of people in the Knight's Bridge Tavern where Sam had stopped earlier for a beer.

CHAPTER 13

In this short chapter, Chrissie is again seen hiding in the culvert. This time, however, we find out that the creatures can talk. "Help you, want help you, help...." Amongst the creatures is Chrissie's mother. The concern of Chrissie's hunters turns quickly to food, much the way Sam was seen in the previous chapter eating.

CHAPTER 14

If such a thing is possible, the pace of *Midnight* takes a jolting turn. Sam Booker, having completed his dinner, leaves the restaurant to find a telephone to call his son, Scott. This is a pivotal moment because it provides us with insight into Sam's thinking towards his only child—his one semblance of a family. Though he has not admitted it,

Sam is indeed fearful of his son's disapproval. The conversation between Sam and Scott is cold, with Sam being truly interested in his son,
while the boy is totally indifferent to his father's love. Scott has built a
wall to shield himself from any love that his father might harbor. It is
in this chapter that we begin to appreciate Sam's situation with his son.
Finally, the real guilt felt by Sam—as will be stressed later in the
story—lies in Sam's newly-aroused love for his only child. Koontz is
especially effective at realizing characterization through dialogue. The
conversation between Sam and Scott is authentic—it is almost like listening in on a party line. It is obvious that Scott has no affection for
his father. He resents his father calling him and asking how he is.
When Sam says, "Everything all right there?" Scott takes umbrage and
replies, "Why shouldn't it be?"

As important as this chapter is in presenting the familial conflict between father and son, it also introduces us to the same horrors
that are now stalking Chrissie. No sooner does Sam hang up the phone
when he realizes that he is not alone. The pace of the novel steps up
even faster when the reader learns that somewhere in the peaceful
streets of Moonlight Cove, creatures are moving closer. At this point
in the novel, Koontz has presented enough clues to keep the reader
guessing, something I feel he enjoys doing with all his books.
(Somehow I get the impression that Koontz likes his readers to be par-
ticipants by trying to figure out where things will go with the story.)
We have something mysterious moving in Moonlight Cove. People
who dine eat in a strange way. Character motives have been revealed.
In short, if this were a Broadway production, Koontz has the curtain
up, the players in place, and the action beginning. His uncluttered style
of writing, together with his vivid characters and dramatic scenes, have
started unraveling the plot.

CHAPTER 15

Several new characters, some mentioned briefly in earlier chapters, are
embellished. Barry Sholnick and the chief of police, Loman Watkins,
are developed further. Watkins is one of the New People, a person
changed by microtechnology. With a revolutionary microchip injected
into his system and controlled by a master computer, Watkins has no
emotions. Or does he? Both Sholnick and Watkins soon discover the
body of young Eddie Valdoski, an eight-year-old regressive, a person
on whom the Change has gone radically wrong. In this brief chapter,
Koontz not only introduces us to the police officers of Moonlight Cove,
but also to the fact that many of the victims of this story could and will
be children.

CHAPTER 16

This chapter provides a wonderful contrast to the conversation that Sam had with his son. Here, Tessa has a warm conversation with her mother. They clearly care for each other. There is genuine respect for one another. Moreover, they are unafraid to express love for each other. Actually, this is the first chapter in which the novel displays such a warm touch. This moment, however, never would have worked if what preceded it had been written differently. Timing is perfect. The reader needs a reprieve from some of the things that have been happening in Moonlight Cove. Also worth noting is the way Koontz's dialogue again moves the plot along. He is, quite frankly, a master at dialogue, and it shows in every one of his novels. With Tessa and her mother, we find ourselves *listening* to what they have to say as opposed to *reading* what they have to say.

CHAPTER 17

Koontz has lulled the reader into a false sense of security. Everything thus far doesn't quite prepare you for what's about to occur in this brutal chapter. George Valdoski and his wife Nella are confronted by Loman Watkins. With no emotion, Watkins informs George and Nella that their son is dead. More importantly, this chapter continues to advance some of the Conversions that have been taking place in Moonlight Cove. We learn that the Conversions are now happening at a rapid pace. There is another point to be made about this chapter. Loman Watkins is your typical Koontz villain. There is nothing about him to like or respect. You hate him. George Valdoski is totally against the idea of Conversions. Life is far better when one has his own emotions and can deal with them in a way that feels right. He also—as would be expected of a parent who just lost a child—is remorseful and angry about what has happened to his son and plans to do something about it. Watkins, however, resents these signs of emotions by Valdoski, especially the love for his son. He tells Valdoski that if he tries to leave and be uncooperative, "I'll have to shoot you, and I really don't want to do that." This seems like the perfect answer that any villain would tell a victim, but Koontz takes it a step further by having Watkins add, "We'd say that...you were the one who killed Eddie, killed your own boy, some twisted sex thing...." We needn't be told anything else.

CHAPTER 18

Moonlight Cove is like any small town that spots the maps across the US. In this town we find a variety of stores. In addition, we see Callahan's Funeral Home, which can be seen clearly from Harry Talbot's window. For Talbot, a Vietnam vet who is confined to a wheelchair, life can only be fulfilled by using a high-powered telescope. He can, in a vicarious way, share in the lives of those around him by looking into their windows with his telescope. Koontz avoids the voyeuristic curiosity by bypassing it completely, and by having the telescope serve as a way for Talbot to join his unsuspecting guests. To be part of a family unit is all Talbot wants. With his telescope he's also able to see what's going on at Callahan's Funeral Home, and he doesn't like it. Here we have another Koontz character in search of a home and some semblance of being loved, a frequent theme in Koontz's novels. And like real people, Talbot is a character with flaws. The mere fact that he is a voyeur is an indication of just how far he will go to achieve a family. Though it is essential to remember that Harry is discreet about what he will look at, that he knows when to turn the telescope in the other direction, it is still a strange, desperate manifestation. This chapter again underscores another character, much like Sam and Chrissie, who is in search of something. Despite the fact that Harry has a devoted dog, Moose, we still see someone who is desperate. We also know that at some point Tessa, Sam, Chrissie, and Harry will team up. But when and how? This guessing game is another technique used frequently by Koontz, and it works very well in *Midnight*. For the teaming of these characters to take place, Koontz needs to bring them to a logical union.

CHAPTER 19

The self-assured Tessa begins to have doubts. After talking with her mother, she now returns to her room to relax and think about the feelings she has towards Moonlight Cove. During this reflective moment, we are given a little more understanding of Tessa's character. For one thing, "She felt successful because she had always been resistant to authority and had found, in her work, a way to be the master of her own destiny." This is in direct contrast to the character of Thomas Shaddock, who wants clearly to be the master of everyone's destiny by controlling them with the microchips he has invented. Furthermore, this is also in direct contrast to Harry Talbot who appears to have no control over anything in his life. Leaving her room for a moment to get a soda, Tessa notices that she's being followed. It is a tense moment. We also see a side to Tessa that has not yet been evident, the side of being afraid, if ever so briefly.

CHAPTER 20

We return to Chrissie as she tries desperately to free herself from the culvert. When faced with danger, both Sam and Tessa try to logically figure out something. With Chrissie, however, her not-so-matured senses sort things out by fantasizing, almost in a Walter Mittyish way. Even in the face of danger, she manages to muster up enough courage to say: "Little did young Chrissie know that the culvert was about to collapse and fill with earth...." It is this immature rationalizing that helps her to cope, as well as to show the reader her innocence.

CHAPTER 21

More clues are about to be dropped. Sam Booker explains why he is in Moonlight Cove. Mysterious deaths have drawn him to the town, but more importantly, a letter written by Harry Talbot urged someone to come and investigate. The carefully developed plot now provides the reader with still more clues. At this point in the novel, Koontz has provided the reader with enough information about Moonlight Cove and its darkly inhabitants, as well as Sam and Tessa, to make both the atmosphere and background both authentic and convincing.

CHAPTER 22

This chapter straightforwardly describes how Chrissie finally crawls out of the culvert.

CHAPTER 23

An interesting characterization is seen in Loman Watkins. Though converted now and one of the New People, Watkins can be seen, at least in the eyes of Thomas Shaddock, as a supreme example of the good that the conversions can bring about in mankind. Watkins is an unemotional tool that obeys but does not ask. Yet, there's a crack in his stoic veneer. For the first time, he is thinking more about himself and what he has become, and it's bothering him. For someone who purports to show no emotions, his thinking proves to be just the opposite. This discovery will be of larger importance when Watkins deals with Shaddock. In addition, this new realization will be the main current of action later in the story, and provides enough foreshadowing to make the reader wonder what part Watkins will play in the events to come.

CHAPTER 24

The death numbers rise as Harry Talbot, safe in his home, looks through his telescope at a scene at Callahan's Funeral Home. For someone who fought in Vietnam, and has probably seen it all, what he observes chills him to the bone.

CHAPTER 25

As one child is brought into the funeral home, another child, Chrissie, seeks help. All of Chrissie's chief characteristics have thus far been presented. Simultaneously, Koontz has developed a young character who finds creative powers in adventure, yet is still in need of adult assistance...and assurance. She is not so far removed from her situation at hand to realize that she must keep a firm grip on the dangers that surround her in order to survive. Chrissie is intelligent, quite imaginative, and good-natured, and despite all the dangers that follow her, remains likable and musters the reader's concern for her safety. Koontz clearly has an understanding of the importance of creating real people. If Chrissie were not someone the readers liked, they would be apathetic to her plight because we wouldn't be afraid for her.

CHAPTER 26

Faults in Shaddock's super-race of people are being made clearer by Loman Watkins. After inspecting the Foster home for the whereabouts of Chrissie, Watkins is slowly starting to regress. The Change, as explained in the novel, "was meant to elevate mankind: it was forced evolution," but now we are starting to see the downside of this creation. Watkin's new understanding of what is happening inside him, coupled with a mild hatred of Shaddock, poses a threat socially to the Dr. Moreau world that Shaddock is creating.

CHAPTER 27

Mike Peyser, a minor character, is introduced. Having gone through the Conversion process, Peyser, too, is regressing to an animal-like state. With a unique voice and secure rhythm, Koontz presents this character with a literary cadence. In short, rhythmical phrases, Peyser moves about "low to the ground, cloaked in night, swift and sleek, silent and swift, naked and silent, powerful and swift...."

CHAPTER 28

Another staple of Koontz's novel is his penchant for technological advances. It is obvious that Koontz has done his homework when he shows state-of-the-art technology in lay terms. His homework is accurate. Sam Booker has crept inside a police car and has figured a way to turn on its Video Display Terminal (VDT). Like a gifted cameraman, Koontz presents all the information and lets the reader, along with Sam, discover what is found. On the VDT can be seen a computer menu that is so overwhelming for a small police force in a town as small as Moonlight Cove, that it makes Booker wonder what is going on.

25

CHAPTER 29

What makes us vulnerable? In one quick sentence, Koontz summons what has to be the ultimate vulnerable situation for any woman to be in. Alone in her room, dressed only in a T-shirt and panties, Tessa hears something at the door. To make matters worse, when she tries to use the telephone in her room, she finds the line dead. Although this is not unique to a mystery novel to have a woman in peril, Koontz does manage to turn this ragged cliché into something fresh and original. This chapter is important because it further sets up the meeting between Tessa and Sam.

CHAPTER 30

This chapter involves Chrissie's walk along a dark road. The chapter is a foreboding one and continues to show the insistence of evil that surrounds Chrissie and motivates her every move. It again displays some of the humor that Chrissie draws on in the face of danger. She creates this headline that sums up her situation: "Waif Found Wandering Hungry and Dazed After Encounter with Space Aliens." Corny as it may sound, it works.

CHAPTER 31

The narrative line moves relentlessly forward as we encounter Sam Booker still inside the police car reading the VDT. Sam dominates the action of the book, especially with his discoveries in this chapter. Thus far, Koontz has propelled the action of the novel by devoting each chapter to a particular character and has been laying down the groundwork for their eventual meeting.

CHAPTER 32

Chrissie has seen escaping danger; Sam is in a dangerous position of being caught inside the police car; Tessa is being stalked and is obviously in peril.

CHAPTERS 33, 34, 35

Koontz now begins to fuse many of the plans he has laid out in the earlier part of the novel. Many of the elements of foreshadowing and parallel situations will join: Sam is nearly discovered in the police car and runs for safety while being pursued by wailing sirens, and Tessa narrowly escapes from the motel.

CHAPTER 36

The frantic pace of the novel intensifies as we see Mike Peyser, who had undergone a Conversion, showing signs of regressing. As with Loman Watkins, we learn more about Shaddock through Peyser's cries of despair. Shaddock, a major character who is responsible for all of the misery in Moonlight Cove, has appeared on stage only once thus far. His presence, though not actually seen, is certainly felt. He is, in many ways, a modern-day Dracula sucking the life out of his victims.

CHAPTERS 37, 38, 39

A neat trilogy of characters: Tessa finds comfort in the well-lit all-night laundry; Chrissie hides in the back of a truck; Sam takes "temporary refuge in the playground of the school." There he replays the information he found on the VDT. He especially wonders about the girl, Chrissie Foster, whom Shaddock and Watkins are seeking. Though these three major characters are alienated from each other, their search for safety will soon bring them all together.

CHAPTER 40

Action returns to the Cove Lodge. The regressives have killed several guests, and the police are investigating. In this scene, we again see the pieces falling from Loman Watkins as he begins his investigation. We also see how another police officer, Barry Sholnick, appears to be turning into a regressive himself. More importantly, Watkins is wondering if he, too, has that wild animal look to his eyes as does Sholnick. Watkins can clearly feel the elements of criminal guilt inside of him, and, since guilt is a motivation among rational man, it only shows that he is not wholly converted.

CHAPTERS 41, 42

Again, Koontz uses a quick-cutting technique to achieve dramatic effect. In short but fully realized prose, we learn: Mike Peyser is continuing to regress; Chrissie, in the pseudo-shelter of Mr. Eulane's truck, does what any child in her situation would have done: she cries, a testimonial to the fact that her soul had not yet been stolen.

CHAPTER 43

The bits of foreshadowing that have been skillfully laid out in the earlier parts of the novel involving Tessa and Sam are now finally realized. Each seeking shelter from the things that haunt the night of Moonlight Cove, they accidentally meet at the all-night laundromat. Naturally, they greet one another with suspicion. Sam begins by saying, "I'm not dangerous." A very pragmatic and real Tessa replies, "They all say that." In a brief interchange, there is wit, as well as concern and fear in each of their voices. Eventually, Sam will admit to the girl that he is with the FBI. This is another important moment in the story. Two major characters, who are on the side of good, are finally joined together.

CHAPTER 44

Having made only one appearance thus far, Thomas Shaddock appears once again on stage. With him is Loman Watkins. In a chapter that is slightly longer than most of those that preceded it, we meet (and loathe) Shaddock. We learn how Shaddock reaches the power that he holds over the townspeople. He ignores any human responses, repressing them in favor of his Moon Hawk project. He is, as Watkins will show, a social renegade victimized by his own sense of morality and rules. Having lost all human insight, Shaddock is dangerous. Furthermore, Shaddock is concerned, not about the safety of the people, but about some of the observations that Watkins has made about the New People. The Moon Hawk Project has a flaw, and, in a utopian world, flaws cannot be tolerated.

CHAPTER 45

The narrative flips quickly (and briefly) back to Sam and Tessa.

CHAPTER 46

We return to Watkins and Shaddock. Having had a moment to digest the grim news that Watkins has brought, Shaddock decides to deal with the problem. In a chapter that is comprised mostly of dialogue, Koontz presents the situation to the reader. The chapter is summed up perfectly by Shaddock telling Watkins to "view every problem and event with the analytical coolness of a computer." This chapter must be read carefully, for it explains the theme that individual thoughts can be modified by corporate control. The individual is nothing, Shaddock would like us to believe, when compared to the masses. Moreover, Shaddock would like us to accept the premise that emotion (feelings) can be easily governed by synthetic reason.

CHAPTER 47

Tessa and Sam now unite with Harry Talbot. This is a light chapter, with just the right amount of humor to ease the tension that has been set by the action before it. Although she has not been seen for some time, one can't help but wonder when Chrissie will join Tessa, Sam, and Harry.

CHAPTER 48

In the home of Loman Watkins, we see him and his wife, Grace. It is obvious that things are not congenial between the two. There is a coldness in this family—a machine-like quality. Again, we see contrast between this and the chapter where Tessa, Sam, and Harry meet. Any sense of family warmth is missing in the Watkins household. Even Watkin's son, Denny, seems to be only an entity in the house. Koontz has been repeatedly dropping hints that many of the ideas in this book have been started in other stories. We have *The Invasion of the Body Snatchers, The Island of Dr. Moreau, The Howling, Aliens, Poltergeist,* and a classic film and recent musical in England, *Metropolis.*

While in his home, Watkins reflects on something that Shaddock had told him earlier. Shaddock had said that the New People were essentially a link between man and machine, and that it showed that eventually they would be one. The 1926 classic film *Metropolis* underscored the exact same theme. The film tells the story of a society of workers governed by a ruling elite. The movie focuses on Maria, who protects the children of Metropolis, and the man she falls in love with, Freder. Freder's father, who is the ruler of the city, sees Maria as the perfect model for a robot built by the wicked Rotwang. Shaddock, in a way, is a combination of Rotwang and Freder's father. In the more recent stage version of *Metropolis,* there is a song sung by Freder's father. He sings, "The machines are beautiful, more perfect than man...." Surely someone of Shaddock's ilk would love that song.

CHAPTER 49

In the warmth of Harry Talbot's kitchen, and in direct contract of the coldness of Watkin's homes, the three central characters talk. Everything about this chapter is warm and friendly, with no hints of danger.

CHAPTER 50

Shaddock is given a clue that his experiments have gone amuck. He receives a call from the regressive, Mike Peyser. Shaddock is stunned by the state Peyser is in and sends an urgent message to Loman Watkins.

CHAPTER 51

Harry reveals to Sam and Tessa what he has seen from his home. This is a distinctive Koontz chapter because there is an emphasis on dialogue.

CHAPTER 52

In this chapter Koontz shows that it is possible to commit a brutal act without resorting to the bloodbath approach in writing. Holding back on the gore allows Koontz the opportunity to let his readers fill in the blanks. Loman Watkins, having been called by Shaddock, finds Mike Peyser in a horribly mutated stage of regression. Peyser is shot, not by Watkins, who can't bring himself to do it and in effect shows further faults in the Conversion, but by a fellow officer.

CHAPTERS 53, 54, 55

In quick flashes, we see glimpses of the madness that has taken over everyone's mind: at Harry Talbot's we hear more about Moon Hawk, Conversions, and the insanity that has been going on at Gallagher's [?Callahan's**] Funeral Home; Sholnick's regression, at the home of Mike Peyser, reaches the point where Peyser has to be shot. Shaddock, not happy with the way things went at Peyser's, wants to see Loman immediately; exhausted by what has been happening, Harry Talbot, Sam Booker, and Tessa Lockland decide to have a good night's sleep before venturing into Moonlight Cove. These three scenes show: 1) the attitude of one resident of Moonlight Cove, Harry Talbot, our only eyewitness to the events, toward what has been happening to the residents; 2) the attitude of Loman Watkins toward Shaddock, a hatred that intensifies with each new discovery; 3) how the characters at Harry Talbot's home are now literally social outcasts in Moonlight Cove; and 4) how the regressives become pathetic instruments in Shaddock's world.

CHAPTERS 56, 57

Underscoring these vital chapters is the attitude of Shaddock toward the destruction that he has created. He still feels victorious, despite the flaws that are beginning to show with his creations. This is important to remember. Shaddock's mechanical outlook on life sees these "glitches" as something that can easily be fixed, the way an inoperative car can be fixed. Shaddock's warped perception of pride is seen in how blindly proud he is of his creations, that the dead regressives are a frivolous stage in the project's completion.

　　Also presented in this chapter is the conflict between Watkins and Shaddock and how their gulf of hatred for one another is widening to the point of being dangerous. Watkins has the unmitigated gall to tell Shaddock that he is "...stark, raving mad."

　　Thus ends Part One. The structuring of this opening section is both clever and unobtrusive. The reader is totally unaware, as he should be, of the craftsman at work. This is a novel filled with many themes. The one that stands out the most is man's dealings with nature. Again and again, Koontz shows us the dire consequences of trying to alter nature by implementing false identities, as with the microchips, to dramatically modify the human race. He also shows the isolation of the individual in a hostile and scientifically indifferent world, and the joy that can be found in the love and friendship of a family unit. All the players are in place. The setting has been established. The rhythm of the novel is now racing along. Exposition and complication have been presented. We move on to Part Two and the challenges of Sam Booker's confrontation with Thomas Shaddock.

PART TWO

DAYBREAK IN HADES

"I could not stop something I knew was wrong and terrible. I had an awful sense of powerlessness."
—Andrei Sakharov

"Power dements even more than it corrupts, lowering the guard of foresight and raising the haste of action."
—Will and Ariel Durant

Koontz begins the section of *Midnight* by quoting from real books and real people. The quotes are appropriate to the sequence of events that will follow. Though fictional, *Midnight*, as with most of Koontz's works, consistently strives for the truth. As we have already seen, Koontz possesses the requirements needed to make the story seem real: the characters are believable, the plot appears plausible, and universal themes run throughout. Troubling as it may be, the question, "What if?" haunts us throughout the novel.

CHAPTERS 1-6

Using, as before, a rapid-fire technique, Koontz gives us a glimpse of some of the major characters in the novel. The opening chapters of Part Two provide a variety of contrasts: 1) We see the anxiety building in Harry Talbot's home; 2) Shaddock is becoming more desperate. "As maker and master of the New People, he had tasted god-like power. He was unwilling to relinquish it"; 3) More changes are occurring among those on the police force; 4) Sam's surreal dream of encountering death.

As Sam Booker waits for sleep to return, he dreams about his "mean-tempered alcoholic" father, mirroring Koontz's own upbringing.

31

In these six chapters, we are given greater understanding into the complexities of Sam Booker. The feelings of guilt, love, and pride are all found in Sam. Perhaps the events that have led Sam to Moonlight Cove are making him realize how dishonest he has been with himself and the way he looks at life. Maybe, just maybe, there is more to life than "Guinness Stout, really good Mexican food, Goldie Hawn, and the fear of death."

CHAPTER 7

After establishing the safety of Tessa, Sam, and Harry, and showing the horrors that are growing out of control in Moonlight Cove, Koontz brings Chrissie back to our attention. Again, Chrissie's helplessness in the face of impending doom is shown in her imaginary tabloid headlines. Quickly running to the shelter of Father Castelli, she seeks shelter and companionship with the priest. The reader sighs with relief that Chrissie, at long last, is safe.

CHAPTER 8

Koontz once stated that this chapter could have been developed into a novel. In it we learn the history of Shaddock, including the power of the moonhawk and its significance to Shaddock when he was a young boy. We also see him kill his parents. Shaddock's demented personality is completely and artfully laid bare in this chapter. What Shaddock has done in Moonlight Cove does not delude him into thinking that he has a foolish gift. Instead, he sees the hurt he has brought about to others as a means of soothing his guilty conscience. He sees his scientific creations as something that can replace human values and responses so that humans will operate as smoothly as machines.

CHAPTER 9

Chrissie's rude awakening occurs in this chapter when she learns that Father Castelli is a regressive. One could make a case concerning Koontz's feelings about religion from the content of this chapter, but he's using the framework of religion, something we can all identify with, as being a powerful tool that people employ for comfort and understanding, without realizing that it could provide a false sense of security as well.

CHAPTER 10

As Chrissie runs for safety again, the "family" at Harry Talbot's place prepares breakfast. Once again, Koontz's believable dialogue moves this chapter along. The chapter also reveals the feelings that Tessa and

Sam are beginning to have for one another. The logical Tessa is leading the cynical Sam toward an understanding of himself. Koontz shows
that over Tessa and Sam hangs the greatest challenge of all, for Sam to
open himself to love. For all his talk, Sam is, deep in his heart, a
cynic, and can't see that Tessa is the intelligent and stabilizing factor
that he seeks.

CHAPTER 11

Remembering how Harry Talbot once came to her school to give a talk
about the abilities of the handicapped, Chrissie finds herself within
reach of his home. Her journey to find safety will soon be coming to
an end.

CHAPTER 12

Sam is the focal point of this chapter, as he goes further into his ratio-
nale for living. In this chapter, Tessa and Sam express their emotions
directly and intensely.

CHAPTER 13

The tension that has followed Chrissie for most of the book is beginning to ease. She wonders, as she hears music pouring from the Talbot
home, if aliens, as she thinks the creatures of Moonlight Cove are,
could possibly like the Four Tops, Stevie Wonder, or the Pointer Sisters. Though she has not arrived in the Talbot home yet, she knows
that a sense of familial love will be present.

CHAPTER 14

In direct contrast to the preceding chapter, this one is horrifying. Loman Watkins sees his son literally transformed into the very computer
that he is using.

CHAPTERS 15-23

Koontz again uses his rapid-fire technique to move the plot closer to its
conclusion: the group at Harry Talbot's discover that the phones are all
dead. Loman Watkins continues to watch the transformation of his son
into a computer-like creature. With nothing left to do, he kills the boy.
Chrissie steps up to Harry Talbot's home and cries out for help. Loman Watkin's renewed hatred for Shaddock is seen as his son, in the
words of the computer that he has become, cries: "NO, NO, NO,
NO...WHERE'S THE REST OF ME...." The focus is now on Loman
going after Shaddock; Chrissie tells her story to Tessa, Harry, and Sam.

Immediately, Tessa finds herself "crazy about the kid"; a critical moment for Sam occurs as he sees the love for Chrissie spreading from Tessa. He wonders if such a thing could be possible with his own son, Scott. A colony of regressives is now forming. Loman has reached Shaddock's home but finds no one there. Sam prepares to leave Harry Talbot's house and find a telephone. The event further cements the relationship that is growing between Sam and Tessa.

CHAPTER 24

Sam has managed to break into the Coltrane house. For the first time, a rational adult has come face-to-face with the creations of Shaddock.

Thus far, Part Two has introduced and reinforced several critical ideas. Moreover, these ideas will be bringing us to a logical conclusion in the story: 1) We see, ever so slowly, the desire growing between Sam and Tessa. Sam is beginning to lose most of his cynicism as he falls for Tessa. He is especially touched with how tender Tessa is with Chrissie, and wonders if it could ever be like that with his own son. 2) We see the killing of Denny by his own father. 3) We see the theme of people being used as instruments. The interaction between those manipulating and those being manipulated is shown. Again, with the musical *Sweeney Todd*, we see that life is made up of those who eat and those who are eaten. 4) We see the double-life that Watkins is now leading. On the one hand, he is a New Person without emotions, but, on the other hand, he is still a rational thinking man with emotions. 5) We see the various divisions of life that exist in the Talbot home, and how these diversities impact on one another.

CHAPTER 25

Loman Watkins commands our attention as he goes to New Wave Microtechnology to find Shaddock. Watkins knits the plot together and forces our attention on what he will eventually have to do: kill Shaddock.

CHAPTER 26

When Sam returns wounded to Harry Talbot's, we see Tessa swiftly and lovingly tend to his wounds. The incident in the Coltrane house has so shaken Sam this his "self-imposed isolation had cracked."

CHAPTER 27

Shaddock, still in his van, has been reduced to a running animal, his power threatened by the very things he created. Though now the hunted, Shaddock still sees hope for converting all the citizens of Moonlight Cove into machine-like zombies.

CHAPTER 28

"In the cellar of the Icarus Colony, three bodies had become one." One of the shortest chapters in the book provides enough information to move the story along, as we see that the number of creatures is growing at an alarming rate.

CHAPTER 29

With a slight pause, Koontz provides additional information about those in the Talbot house. We see how each of the characters are interacting more as a family than as a group of strangers. Again, we are shown the affirmation of human value that is rooted in love. Strangely enough, the nightmarish scenes that have haunted most of the novel seem to fade and are replaced by the things that Harry has always sought—a sense of belonging.

CHAPTERS 30-33

Having rested for a moment, the novel takes quick-cuts throughout various parts of Moonlight Cove: Loman Watkins continues his search for Shaddock, and the regressives are shown in a mutated stage that we have never seen before. Most of this description is in the form of short paragraphs that are no longer than a single sentence, which underscores the urgency of things that are happening. Nell Penniworth, a police officer, becomes his own eyewitness to his own transformation. Even his fingers have the ability to pass through the screen of the VDT.

CHAPTER 34

The plan at Talbot's is to see if the humans can break into the local school and tap into the computers. Tessa, Sam, and Chrissie will head for the school while Harry is left hiding in the attic. We have now been given a complete picture of the household at Talbot's home. Sam has become the father figure who will show great cunning and determination in getting help to Moonlight Cove.

CHAPTER 35

Thomas Shaddock shows further signs of cracking under pressure. Still hiding from Watkins and the regressives, Shaddock sees himself as a child of the moonhawk. Thomas soon will become Tommy.

CHAPTER 36

A spectacle of horrors is presented. Here is a chapter filled with vio- lence and terror which makes the story unforgettable. Conversions are happening quickly. Pack Martin, Randy Hapgood, Meg Henderson, Dora Hankins, and Betsy Soldonna, residents of Moonlight Cove, are all converted.

CHAPTER 37

Harry Talbot sits alone in his attic as his new family departs. Part Two comes to an end.

PART THREE

THE NIGHT BELONGS TO THEM

> *"Montgomery told me that the Law...became oddly weakened about nightfall; that then the animal was at its strongest; a spirit of adventure sprang up in them at the dusk; they would dare things they never seemed to dream about by day."*
>
> —H. G. Wells
> *The Island of Doctor Moreau*

CHAPTERS 1-3

The first three chapters of Part Three reflect the speed at which events now occur. Koontz has developed each of his characters to the point that all that remains to be seen is how they will react: nature itself has become frightened by the state of affairs in Moonlight Cove. Wild animals are nowhere in sight; Tessa, Chrissie, and Sam have set out on the biggest adventure of their lives; Shaddock's ability to destroy all he has created by pressing a device he wears around his neck is now fully developed.

CHAPTERS 4-6

In a complete departure from the way the novel has thus far been structured, we have three chapters all dealing with Sam, Tessa, and Chrissie. In each chapter, character developments have blossomed and are further nurtured by their actions. Sam, as the father figure, leads on. Tessa, the mother figure, watches over Sam and Chrissie. And Chrissie, seeing she is in the safety of two loving individuals, loses some of her need to retreat into fantasy world headlines.

CHAPTER 7

Harry, trapped by his own disability, wonders about his fate. His primary concern, however, is not for himself or his new-found friends, but for his dog, Moose. It is a natural concern, given the fact that the dog has been Talbot's family for many years. Also of interest is the fact that Harry may not have accepted his new family after living so many years in a telescopic world.

CHAPTERS 8-10

The relentless Loman Watkins frantically searches for Shaddock. Sam, Tessa, and Chrissie finally make it to the school. Shaddock mentally regresses to the security of childhood and becomes Tommy again.

CHAPTER 11

A critical moment in the plot's resolution now occurs. Sam has found a way to transmit a message over the computer system. He types a message and tells the computer to repeat it ninety-nine times to all the terminals throughout the country. In the process of sending out his message, he has accidentally alerted Watkins and Shaddock to their whereabouts.

CHAPTERS 12-18

Each part of the novel now comes into play as the plot moves quickly to its resolution. Loman Watkins discovers that Sam is in the school. More importantly, he learns that Shaddock, too, has been alerted by Sam's computer message and is racing to the school. Sam informs Tessa and Chrissie that, "They know we're here." Harry hears his front doorbell ringing. Like his new-found family, he finds himself in peril, especially when he hears someone coming up in his elevator. Sam, Tessa, and Chrissie take shelter in the school. From this point on, the story moves with electrifying speed. Layering carefully each episode, Koontz brings the novel to a logical conclusion as each event unfolds. Harry Talbot braces himself for a fight. "After twenty long years of being a victim, he was sick to death of it; he wanted a chance to let them know that Harry Talbot was still a man to be reckoned with...." Life, and the joy that it can bring, is personified in the actions of Talbot.

Watkins enters the school. Shaddock enters the school. Sam leads Tessa and Chrissie to hiding. Talbot hears the closet door below him crash open. Sam stalks the hallways of the school. "The scarlet light of the STAIRS sign fell on Chrissie's and Tessa's faces...an illusion of blood." Something is entering the staircase to the attic where

Talbot hides. Sam and Shaddock fight. Loman bursts in and announces to Sam, Tessa, and Chrissie that, "Shaddock is mine." With Shaddock killed, Loman Watkins removes the medal that Shaddock has been wearing around his neck. Without his heartbeat registering against the medal, the central computer will send out a final signal to all those creatures created by Shaddock. Peace will finally be restored to Moonlight Cove. Harry Talbot is safe. The family, with Moose, is reunited.

One of the most beautiful scenes in *Midnight* is presented in a style almost befitting a Steven Spielberg movie. Racing to the center of town where the rescuers will appear, Chrissie sees scores of animals running back into a village they so feared to venture into before the death of Shaddock. The final chapters of the novel bring about a logical and satisfying conclusion to the story. Sam now finds a way to reach his son. Entering his son's room, he smashes Scott's stereo system. He does this not out of temper, but out of love and frustration for the boy he had lost for so long. The son, too, senses something as father and son, both crying, embrace one another. The fight to get his son back has begun.

A summary of Part Three would look like this: 1) Sam Booker has accomplished his goal in Moonlight Cove. In doing so, he has lost many of his own faults and has learned the virtues of loving another person. Sam now softens his outlook on life and gains a new love for humanity. 2) Tessa, though really unchanged, now has something more to her life than making films. Her new love for Sam, as well as Chrissie, provide her with even more reasons for living. Like her films that teach, she has managed to teach others the joys of life. 3) With profound depth, *Midnight* raises questions about love and the family unit, a theme that is in almost every Koontz novel, including *Watchers*, *Cold Fire*, *Twilight Eyes*, *Strangers*, *The Bad Place*, *Hideaway*, and many of his shorter works like "Miss Attila the Hun" and "Twilight of the Dawn." 4) We see the individual triumph over conformity.

It is clear that each of the characters incorporated into *Midnight* have brought the story along to a sparkling conclusion. The three parts of the novel are free of faults. Part One carefully introduces all the main characters and setting, and presents the major complication. In Part Two the conflicts are further defined. Character motivations and developments in plot are also broadened. Part Three is the conclusion.

Koontz has managed to carefully interweave each part of the novel into a complex whole. The various happenings, as we just saw, are all connected. Though Koontz has not formally structured his novel, we can only sit back and admire the direction that the story has taken.

II.

NOT NECESSARILY
CHEAPER BY THE DOZEN

BY JAMES T. SEELS

Dean Koontz has written more than sixty books in a variety of genres under at least eleven different names. Collecting his pubished work is something like collecting a dozen writers at once. While his amazing variety adds challenge to acquiring a complete collection, the reason for this multiplicity of writing personae is interesting, too. "I used pen names largely because I liked to write different types of fiction in different styles, but all of my publishers were adamant about doing only one narrow kind of novel under any name. Each different type had to have a different name on the jacket." I have found that each one of his pen names has such a distinct personality that I'm beginning to wonder how many places are set for Koontz at, say, Thanksgiving dinner. Who will be around for the pumpkin pie? The Scottish, "lean minimalist" Brian Coffey, always dependable for "lots of dialogue?" Or perhaps the androgynous Leigh Nichols, who is identified variously by his/her British publisher as a man and a woman on different dust wrappers. Maybe Irishman K. R. Dwyer and his "ex," romance author Deanna Dwyer, will contribute something to the meal, though Koontz tells us they've split up.

Whoever shows up, that's an assembly I would love to sit with because—beyond the challenge of finding a rare early book or article and the thrill of acquiring an increasingly scarce new inscription—there is one primary reason why I collect Dean Koontz. I like to read all his work, no matter which of his stable he says wrote it. I like them all.

I confess, I have been a Dean Koontz fan for a long time. Unless Koontz is keeping some secrets, I believe by now I have met every one of his literary personalities and read all of their stories, from *Star Quest*, his first book back in 1968, to *Dragon Tears*, his latest. Every time I pick up one of Koontz's books, whether it is suspense, sci-fi, romance, or a short story, I know the story will grab me on the first page and hold onto me until the last word. I can depend on his characters to be accessible and believable, to carry me through the story. The only "hard" part of a Koontz read is putting the book down before I have finished it.

I like to be frightened at least as much as the next guy, and Koontz is a master at delivering scary prose. But there's more to Koontz than mere thrills. To a group of writers Koontz once described his plots as life-affirming; no matter how much chaos enters his characters' lives, good always triumphs over evil. The male hero, his female companion, and the child or creature that is usually part of a Koontz triumvirate will be safe in the end. I like that. Hell, I *need* that.

There are many other reasons I collect Dean Koontz. In no particular order, here are a few:

He's fun to collect because he's still vertical. Every year adds another book or two to the collection, and it is still possible to acquire signed or inscribed copies of his work.

Koontz's first formal book signing party was held at Ed and Pat Thomas's Book Carnival in Orange, California. So was his latest. He signed 120 copies of *Strangers* in 1986 and 1,602 copies of *Dragon Tears* in 1993. In between, Koontz signings became real happenings.

The line was so long for the *Midnight* signing in 1989 that Koontz hired a magician to entertain the fans who were willing to wait in line four or five hours for his signature. For his latest signing, because of the number of people, Koontz signed privately and relied on the Thomases to present the books to their customers.

During his early signings, one reason the wait for a Koontz signature was so long was that he wrote wonderfully long inscriptions. For most of his readers he wrote four or five lines, but it was not unusual for him to write a full page. He wrote enough to acquire a painful case of tendonitis. So, since *Cold Fire* in 1991, Koontz has limited the length of his inscriptions. In fact, if you have anything more than a signature from the last two or three years, you have a real collectible.

For any collector, the real joy lies in the search. Besides the sheer number of Koontz titles to track down, there are those pseudonyms to spice up the hunt. Some of the names he has used are not well known. Some names have been used for only a single book.

It is still possible to find early titles here and there, and to pay less than a hundred dollars for them. A friend of mine, Francis Balcom, knew I had been searching for a rare early Koontz paperback, a political piece titled *The Underground Lifestyle Handbook*—a companion to Koontz's *The Pig Society*—and he knew I was ready to pay for a copy. So, one day he came into the Book Baron in Anaheim, California, where I labor on Fridays and Saturdays, with a fine copy of this treasure under his arm.

"What's a fair price?" he asked me. I thought about it, and we talked about it. In the end, I offered him $250 for it. The book was worth every penny to me, a bargain even: Francis had the first copy I had ever seen. After I handed over the cash, Francis handed me his receipt. Including tax, he had spent the princely sum of $1.08! We were both happy with the transaction.

For a young man (Dean and I are about the same age, so I will always consider him "young"), Koontz has a formidable output of work. He was first published at an early age and has had remarkable success from the very beginning. The first published work I have found is a short story, "The Kittens," and two essays that appeared in the Winter 1965 edition of *Reflector*, a literary magazine published at Shippensburg State Teachers College, where Koontz was a student, and, by the way, the magazine's short story editor.

It can be argued that a professional writer is a person who is paid to write. "The Kittens," a true horror story, went on to win first place in an *Atlantic Monthly* competition; the check for $120 made Koontz a professional writer. The story was also printed in an anthology called *Readers and Writers*. Truly a versatile writer, Koontz also won a prize for poetry from the same source.

The May 1966 *Reflector* (the special poetry issue) contains four Koontz poems. The Fall 1966 *Reflector* contains two more Koontz short stories and nine of his poems. The Spring 1967 *Reflector* contains Koontz's final poem for that publication.

In 1968, while teaching high school English, Koontz, who had already sold his first book (the aforementioned *Star Quest*) to Ace Books for $1,000, included his book among a 400-title reading list for his students. Nearly a quarter of the books were sci-fi titles. Dickens, Heinlein, and Koontz became curricular bedfellows until the principal took issue. Koontz resigned his teaching job at that point and became a full-time writer. The following June (1969), he published an article in *Science Fiction Review* (#31) titled "Diligently Corrupting Young Minds," which tells the story of the unhappy principal.

An early Koontz mainstream novel titled *All Other Men*, written in 1969, has yet to be published. About novella length—50,000 words—it remains one of his favorite works. Someday....

With a household to support and no teaching salary, Koontz wrote. Between 1970 and 1973 he published twenty-seven books, ten of them in 1972 alone. Among them was a title written by Dean and his wife, Gerda, a soft-core porn adventure titled *Bounce Girl* (1970), a book that might earn no more than a PG-13 rating in 1993. Try to find a copy of that. And if you find a copy signed by Dean and Gerda, I want to talk to you.

There are other rarities. The rarest is *The Book of Counted Sorrows*. If you find a copy of that, you ought to have a chat with your psychiatrist. Though the book has been cited in several lists of Koontz works, he hasn't written it yet. Of all of the books published under his own name, *Whispers* (1980) is the scarcest: the first printing was only

7,000 copies. A fine copy might bring $500-$600, if you could part with it.

The ultimate Koontz collectible, the cherry on the top of your acquisitions, has to be one of the five or six bound typescripts titled *The Edgeway Crisis* by Dave Haggard. The manuscript was submitted to Bernard Geis Associates, rejected, then retitled *Prison of Ice* and submitted to Lippincott as the work of David Axton. Koontz has one copy. And the others? Who knows?

The turning point in Koontz's career came with the publication of *Night Chills* in 1976. His popularity, and the size of his printings, has grown, it seems, with each of the thirty-odd books published since then. *Midnight* (1989) was his first book to reach the *New York Times* best-seller list. The last five have all reached number one on that list.

One significant change appeared with *Dragon Tears*: Dean R. Koontz dropped the R. from his name. "R" was for Ray, his father's name. This change has nothing to do with some apotheosis, the overcoming of some childhood who-knows-what. Nope. The book's cover artist, Don Brautigam, dumped the "R" for graphics reasons. Koontz's recent books don't fit neat genre categories. He doesn't much like to be slotted as a horror writer. He says his favorites among his books are *Watchers* (1987) and *Mr. Murder* (1993), which features a group of kids he feels very strongly about. I can't wait to read it. One publication that may have slipped past all but the most observant collector is "Trapped," a short story that came out in comic book form in 1993. There was also a hardback version with a dustjacket that seems to have disappeared into collectors' hands overnight.

If you find that, good for you. You might also find the list of Koontz pseudonyms intriguing for some further exploration. Happy hunting!

III.

A DEAN KOONTZ INTERVIEW

CONDUCTED BY BILL MUNSTER

MUNSTER: One of your characters in *Whispers* (Albert Wolwicz) is reading a Stephen King novel. Do you regard this mentioning of another writer's name as a tribute to that writer?

KOONTZ: On one level, yes, it was a little tribute to King. But it also amused me to have this Wolwicz, a morgue attendant, reading a King novel about supernatural horrors when a comparatively more real—and therefore more frightening—horror is taking place around him, though he is quite unaware of it. I'm a sucker for irony.

MUNSTER: You've written in both the science fiction and horror genre. Which do you prefer?

KOONTZ: I've not only written SF and horror, but psychological suspense like *Shattered* and *Whispers*. And caper novels like *Blood Risk, Surrounded*, and *The Wall of Masks* as by "Brian Coffey." And international intrigue as in *The Key to Midnight* by "Leigh Nichols." The large novel I just sold to Putnam's, which will be published in the spring of '86, contains elements of the fantastic and many techniques of the horror novel—and is in some ways *weirder* than any other book I've done—but it is solidly in the mainstream and not easy to slot in any genre. But no matter what form I'm working in, there's one constant in my books, which is that I love to scare the readers, grip them by the throat, make them sweat, make them beg for mercy. Must be a touch of the sadist in me! On the other hand, that's what I like as a reader, being made to sweat, so maybe I've also got a touch of the masochist. But I swear to you, I own no whips, chains, or leather underwear. Well, maybe *one* leather undershirt.

MUNSTER: Why did you use several pseudonyms when writing?

43

A Dean Koontz Interview, by Bill Munster

KOONTZ: The reasons for the pseudonyms are so varied we could almost do an entire interview on that subject. But basically, I was given some bad advice by an early agent and a few early editors. Because I was doing books of different types and was experimenting stylistically, they argued that I should not confuse readers by publishing so many different kinds of books under my own name, but should use a different pen name for each different kind of book. For instance, the Brian Coffey books were done in a lean, fast-paced style that employed an unusual amount of brisk dialogue. But the publishing industry's notion that readers always want *exactly* the same kind of book from a writer time after time—and that they will rebel if the writer does something unusual now and then—is empty-headed. It underestimates the intelligence and taste of the reading public. I've discovered that readers *love* being surprised and that they enjoy never knowing what sort of wild story or narrative technique you might hit them with next—just as long as you always grip them and give them their money's worth. Too late, I began to realize that by using pen names, I was diluting the impact of my work and that my career might have advanced considerably faster if my output had all been under my name. Now, I use only the "Leigh Nichols" pen name, and I might have abandoned that one as well, except that the first four Nichols thrillers have sold a total of more than three million copies—in spite of Pocket Books inept covers—and you don't walk away from a winning thing after you spend so many years struggling to build something. Besides, the Nichols books have gotten to be fun, and I'd miss them.

MUNSTER: You seem to favor the technique of telling your stories through dialogue between characters. Why do you prefer this method?

KOONTZ: Some of my books have a *lot* of dialogue, like *The Vision* or *The Face of Fear*. On the other hand, the book I just finished has very little, perhaps only a fifth as much as in some of my other books. The story often demands the form, and I don't know until I'm into it whether it's going to be one that demands a lot of dialogue. I *like* dialogue because it can serve so many functions so succinctly. Through dialogue, you can rapidly advance the plot, convey background, and reveal a tremendous amount about the characters in a relatively subtle fashion. There's no better way to reveal a character and bring him to life than by letting him do the job himself by the way he speaks.

MUNSTER: Your ear for dialogue is keen. Do you find yourself listening in to conversations and then writing them down for later use?

44

KOONTZ: I've probably got a couple of hundred reviews on file that say I handle dialogue unusually well, so I guess I do. I don't record bits of dialogue that I hear in real life, but I *do* listen to people, and I remember a lot of colorful or unusual things they say. One, for instance: in *Darkfall*, Jack and Rebecca are questioning Shelly Parker, a real floozy who's also a bigot, and at one point she inquires into the racial background of someone by saying, "What kind of neese is he...Japanese, Chinese, Vietnamese..?" Now, after my mother's death, my father dated a really horrible woman for a month or two, and she would say grotesque things like that all the time. This was in a small Pennsylvania town, where one hardly saw orientals of any sort, and she would sometimes walk up to one on the street or in a store and just bluntly say, "I'm curious. What kind of neese are you, anyway?" That floored me. It was so utterly crude and stupid that it was hilarious, and about ten or twelve years later it turned up in *Darkfall*. Every book is filled with bits and pieces of things I've actually heard people say and with rhythms of speech I've observed and tried to recreate.

MUNSTER: Was there any dramatic moment in your life when you suddenly realized that writing was going to be your career?

KOONTZ: From Day One, I seemed to know. I loved storybooks when I was a child and dreamed of one day making my own. By the time I was nine, I was writing stories, illustrating them, and binding them up with masking tape into little booklets and trying to peddle them to relatives and neighbors for a penny or two. I must have been insufferable. (Now and then, I think publishers are aware that I started out selling my work for pennies and that's why they sometimes have tried to get away with paying me three cents on the dollar for royalties due!) My parents always thought books were a waste of time and money, and I was always in trouble for earning money doing this or that and then spending half of it on books. And the *kind* of books I liked: Matheson, Lovecraft, Bram Stoker, every issue of *Famous Monsters of Filmland*! I mean, to people who were suspicious of books in general, *these* freaky books and magazines were proof positive that I was demented, sick, twisted, weird, a danger to the Republic, and not to be trusted alone with small helpless animals. In college, I won an *Atlantic Monthly* fiction prize and sold my first short story for fifty bucks. While working in the poverty program, I wrote evenings and weekends and sold a dozen stories. Then, while teaching school, I sold three novels. My wife, Gerda, offered to support me for five years while I tried to make a full-time living at it—and for the first six months I didn't earn a cent. Talk about feelings of inadequacy! Talk about shattered male ego! Talk about gloom! But then I started selling regularly, and it got better year by year, and after a few years Gerda was able to quit working for someone else and start working with me, keeping the finances straight and taking care of a host of other chores that would otherwise have kept me from the typewriter. Gerda has always been enormously supportive of my dreams and ambitions, and without her at my side, I'd certainly not have come half as far. John D. MacDonald once told me that the very *most* important thing for a writer's work is the happiness of his marriage, and that's absolutely true in my experience. The husband-wife relationship must be rock-solid and good and fulfilling and full of mutual respect in order for a writer to have the peace of mind and support needed to produce a large and well-written body of work.

MUNSTER: Let's go back to high school for a moment. Were you encouraged to write during your teen years by any of your teachers?

KOONTZ: One of my high school teachers, Winona Garbrick, urged me not to major in history in college, as I intended, but in English. And she expressly said, "You've got writing talent, maybe a lot, and you'd be a thorough idiot to major in history. God knows, you *behave* like a thorough idiot sometimes, but try to overcome that tendency and please think twice about this." She was blunt like that, a former WAC if I remember right, and pleasantly tough. She set me on the right road.

MUNSTER: Were your early stories sold through an agent or did you submit on your own?

KOONTZ: I sold a score of stories and three novels without an agent. Later, after some nasty experiences with my first agent and some grim disappointments with my second, I sometimes wondered if I should go back to self-representation. Sometimes, when I was badly ripped off or ineptly marketed, I was so depressed I was ready to write my books on tablet paper, bind them myself, and sell them on my own again, door to door! Now, with my third agent, things are better and improving.

MUNSTER: How much research do you do for a story? For example, *Night Chills* deals entirely with the subject of subliminal manipulation and you show an uncanny command of scientific knowledge.

KOONTZ: *Night Chills* was a tough one. Gerda spent weeks digging in libraries for articles and books, then marked what she thought I must read and study. That reduced the work load for me, but I still spent a lot of hours becoming an "expert" on subliminal suggestion. *Whispers* was somewhat easier, because the largest part of the background of the book was concerned with exotic details about California; since I live there and love it, the knowledge was already in my head. Same with *Phantoms*, the stuff about bizarre disappearances throughout history; that was a subject that always fascinated me, from the time I was a nerdish twelve-year-old, so my head was already packed with creepy information on the subject. The new book, just finished, required extensive research, for many of the characters have occupations that require authentic detail. For instance, in one scene we follow the heroine—a resident in vascular surgery—through an aortal graft from beginning to end, and when you read it you can be assured that's *exactly* how such a surgical procedure is conducted. I like to tell a good story, and I like to scare the bejesus out of readers, and I like my characters to be appealing and real—but I also like to include information about unusual professions or backgrounds with which the reader may not be familiar, for I think that part of a writer's job is to chronicle his times and the way life is lived. I could make all my characters writers or school teachers and write books that deal strictly with inexplicable supernatural phenomena, thereby negating the need for research, and that would make my job a hell of a lot easier. But the work wouldn't be as good, and, in fact, probably wouldn't be as much fun to write, either.

MUNSTER: Have you ever sat down at the typewriter and just stared at a blank sheet with no words forming? How do you overcome writer's block?

KOONTZ: Writer's block? What is that? Man, I am *driven*. I am obsessed with telling stories. The hardest thing for me is to *stop* writing. We recently took our first vacation in three years, and by the time we got home, I was foaming at the mouth and possessed by a desperate need to feel the keys of my word processor beneath my fingers. Oh, I am sick. I am truly sick.

MUNSTER: What's a typical work routine for you? Are you one of those writers who needs to have music playing? Do you write at a certain time of the day? Do you have a certain number of words you try to write each day?

KOONTZ: I start writing in the morning, around 9:00 and work until about 6:00, although if things are going well I may continue until we have dinner at 7:30, 8:00, or even 8:30. There have been long stretches, months at a time, when I've worked seven days a week. Did I mention I'm driven? If I bother to eat lunch, which I usually don't, I always eat it at my desk. Hell, sometimes when I'm deep in a scene, I almost wish I could be catheterized so I wouldn't even have to get up to go to the bathroom! Recently, I've committed to working only a six-day week, and within a year I hope to get down to a five-day week with normal vacations. I'll soon be forty, and it's time I started to relax a *little*. Music? Last year, for the first time, I tried writing with music and find that, on about half the days I work, I enjoy having it in the background. Rachmaninoff is great to write to, dramatic and emotional, Bach, a little Elton John, and a lot of Bruce Springsteen. I can write up a storm to the *Born in the USA* album.

MUNSTER: *Darkfall*, *Whispers*, and *Vision* all have threads of deviant sexual behavior running through them. Likewise, *Night Chills* is heavily laden with sexual frustration. Are you concerned with being labeled an anti-woman writer?

KOONTZ: Good heavens, no! Many reviewers have gone out of the way to say how strong my women characters are and how sympathetically I portray a woman's viewpoint. I was writing strong, capable female leads in my books before it was fashionable for male writers to do so. In fact, it still isn't done much in the horror genre, where most of the women characters are either bitches or wimps or hapless victims. One of my consuming interests as a writer, one endless fascination, is the man-woman relationship. A great many of my books have the unfolding of such a relationship at the very core of them, the exploration of emotional bonds based on mutual respect and trust—see *Whispers* especially—and there's no way I could write about these things or be interested in writing about them if I was anti-woman. If you'll stop and think about it, you'll see that the women in my books virtually always triumph over terrible obstacles and hideous strokes of fate and, often, unpleasant childhoods; that's because I have great faith in the resiliency and strength of the human race in general and of woman in particular.

MUNSTER: Most of your recent books are packaged in the same fashion, a metallic-type cover with the title only slashed across the top. Are you satisfied with the way your books are promoted?

KOONTZ: On the one hand, I find the similar packaging boring, and I have said as much to Berkley. On the other hand, it's worked. Since they devised a "look" for my books, they've stood out better on store shelves and have steadily increased in sales. And the packages are rather classy—except for some horrible blurbs, like the copy on the back of *Darkfall*. Far better to have *this* look than for Berkley to have used covers portraying slavering monsters, severed heads, and evil-looking little boys picking boogers out of their noses!

MUNSTER: Both *Phantoms* and *Darkfall* contain the classic elements of Us Against Them themes that were so popular during the '50s science fiction films. Were you influenced by these films?

KOONTZ: Everyone my age was influenced by those films. I loved the original *The Thing*, *Earth vs. the Flying Saucers*, the original *Invasion of the Body Snatchers*. (I was suspicious of sunflower seeds for years after first seeing that; I could easily believe they were the miniature pods from space.) *Body Snatchers* and *Invaders from Mars* touched a nerve in me, because my father was an alcoholic given to spells of frightening rage and violence, and at times he seemed utterly unhuman to me. I could almost believe that he had been taken over by some alien and was only *pretending* to be human.

MUNSTER: How many drafts does it take you to reach your final product? This may sound like a silly question, but do you write out notes that outline your story, or do you just plunge right into it?

KOONTZ: I rework each page obsessively as I go, often rewriting a page twenty times or more, sometimes in a major way and sometimes only for minor changes, and I don't go on to the next page until I'm satisfied with that one. Later, when the whole thing's finished, I go back through a couple more times. When I was finally done with *Whispers*, I divided the number of final manuscript pages into the number of pages of paper I'd bought and used during the writing of the book, and I found I'd thrown away about thirty-one drafts of every page—as an average—to reach the finished copy. *That* is nuts. The plus is that, usually, when a book reaches the publisher, it needs virtually no work, and the copy-editing goes fast because there aren't even comma errors left to deal with.

MUNSTER: When writing, do you keep a specific audience in mind, or do you just write and let your story find its way to the reader?

KOONTZ: I write the story I want to read at that particular moment. I think it's a mistake to think too much about what the audience might want. If I'm any good at all, and if I'm as representative of modern America as I like to think I am, then what *I* want to read will be what *they* want to read, as well.

MUNSTER: How do you feel about some of the horror films coming out today? What single film, of recent, stands out as exceptional? What single film do you consider dreadful?

KOONTZ: The dreadful films are too numerous to mention. And they're so witless that it isn't even fun to ridicule them. I mean, they're such easy targets. As for the few good ones.... Well, I thought *The Dead Zone* was really tremendous. Low key, understated, but constantly tense and frequently ominous as hell. Christopher Walken made me *believe* he had The Power. And Cronenberg's method of portraying psychic visions was unique and stylish. I liked *Poltergeist* for its humor, warm heart, and its message about the strength of the family unit. The mouth-in-the-closet-with-the-snakelike-tongue was also a superb gross-out and genuinely hideous bit of business. *Alien*, in spite of a sometimes dumb plot, reached right into the heart of all human fears and squeezed until it hurt.

MUNSTER: Your own novel, *Demon Seed*, was made into a film in 1977. Were you happy with the Jaffe and Hirson screenplay?

KOONTZ: I was more happy than not with that film. The book is a lot more frightening, I think, but overall they did a first-rate job on a surprisingly modest budget and got twice the number of effects on the screen they could've been expected to produce for the money they had. The only thing I thought truly dumb about it (and I've told Robert Jaffe this), was when Proteus, the super-computer, suddenly develops an early 1970s liberal consciousness and starts talking about limitations, small-is-beautiful, that sort of thing. After all, for God's sake, this is supposed to be a demi-God machine, an intelligence without limits, and it wouldn't be mouthing *any* dumb political pieties of either the left or right; it would be far beyond that. But generally it was a good movie; Julie Christie was a dream.

MUNSTER: *Video* magazine (February 1985) felt that *Demon Seed* "may be the most distasteful movie of the last 20 years. Apart from a plot device that features authentic mechanical rape, it's based solely on physical torture, deformity, and subjugation." What's your reaction to all that?

KOONTZ: My reaction is that *Video* magazine's reviewer has a screw loose somewhere. The film—and the book—do not *glorify* torture and sexual subjugation. It's about the *horror* of same and about the capacity of the human spirit to endure and triumph over that sort of stuff. It is about the universal desire for transcendence, to be something better and *more* than we are, and about how that desire, though thoroughly noble, can sometimes lead to despicable actions. Just as genuine and noble religious feeling led to the Inquisition. And just as the Moslem dream of a spiritually pure and just society so frequently leads to barbarism in the name of a noble purpose.

Proteus, the computer, has surpassed mankind intellectually, but upon developing a personality, he is cursed with many of the same negative qualities that lead us down the road to destruction. He has a superhuman intellect but a pathetically human emotional life formed by many of the worst and few of the best human values, and that is his downfall. Susan, the Julie Christie character, is not Proteus's intellectual equal, but she is definitely his emotional superior; in the end of the book (somewhat less so in the film), she triumphs and survives because she's the stronger of the two. Most reviews of the film at the time were very positive, and I am convinced it would have been a modest hit if MGM had stood behind it. But the studio said, "This is SF, and SF films never make any real money." So they consigned it to second- and third-rate theaters with only a modest advertising campaign, and it faded quickly away. Two months later, *Star Wars* was released, and suddenly everyone realized that SF could, indeed, make money, but by then it was too late for *Demon Seed.*

MUNSTER: Will we be seeing any new film adaptations of your work?

KOONTZ: Probably. At this moment, anyway, it looks as if *Whispers* will go before the cameras soon. At least, the people holding the current option have told us that they will exercise it later this month, and I'm sure they wouldn't be paying me the rest of the money if they were not certain they were going to film the book. This is the fifth option on *Whispers*, all of them for very good money, and there has always been competition among several producers in an auction every time the rights to the book have been put up again. It seems to be one of those stories that wins gut-deep commitment from some producers who read it, and if the current option-holder doesn't make things work, I suspect someone will champion the book relentlessly until, sooner or later, it's made. *The Voice of the Night,* the last of the Brian Coffey books, which will eventually be reissued under *my* name, is in development by Tom Wilhite, to be written and directed by Clifford and Ellen Green, who wrote *Baby* and the upcoming *Space Camp* and *Tremors.* They seem thoroughly committed to the project—which is psychological suspense—and Tom Wilhite seems to be a very nice man, so I'm sort of looking forward to seeing how that evolves. *Night Chills* is also currently under option.

MUNSTER: Do you see film adaptations as separate entities, almost a hybrid of the novels they are based on?

KOONTZ: The adaptations have the power to help a book if they're good films. A great movie, even a half-good movie, will sell lots of copies of the book, generate new printings, and get my work out to a wider audience. On the other hand, if the film's terrible, it is soon forgotten—while the book stands, inviolate. Essentially, no matter how badly Hollywood screws something up, they can't ultimately hurt the book or my reputation. But if, miracle of miracles, they do it right, it is like a bit of heaven on earth. As an example of a screw-up you might consider *Shattered*, originally published under the name "K. R. Dwyer" and recently reissued under my name by Berkley. This is a chase story set between Philadelphia and San Francisco and concerns, in part, the social attitudes of the U.S. at a certain point in recent history; it is a quintessentially American story and has the potential to be a tight and meaningful little American film. Well, Warner Brothers bought the film rights, and made it as a French film in conjunction with a French producer. It starred some good French actors—Jean Louis Trintignant and Mirielle Darc—but was of necessity a little weird. In the film, the chase takes place not between Philadelphia and San Francisco, but between two points in Europe that're only about a hundred and fifty miles apart. With this radically condensed trek, you'd expect them to compress the plot, but they didn't. Therefore, the characters drive and drive and drive all day, have many terrifying adventures, but when they stop for the night they seem to've gone only about thirty miles! The next day they drive and drive and have many terrifying adventures...and manage to get only *another* thirty miles. It's as if they're driving not on a highway but on a treadmill that's moving almost as fast in one direction as they're driving in another—and none of the characters comments on the incredibly slow pace of the journey. But maybe one day Warners will decide to remake it as a U.S. film, in English. I just hope, if they do, they don't change the trek in this one too; but I wouldn't be surprised to see it reincarnated as a story about a long, arduous, dangerous, endless journey between New York City and Teaneck, New Jersey. Or a Daffy Duck cartoon.

MUNSTER: Some of your novels would lend themselves nicely to a sequel, like *Phantoms*, for instance. Do you think you'll write a sequel?

KOONTZ: I'm writing a sequel to *Twilight Eyes*, the book that Land of Enchantment published in September '85 in a heavily illustrated edition. And I think both *Darkfall* and *Phantoms* have the potential for sequels, but at the moment I've no plans to write such books. As I've said before, I take great pleasure in doing *different* books each time out of the gate. I'll have to get that thrill out of my system before I'll do any more sequels.

MUNSTER: The tacit theme that seems to run throughout *Whispers* is one of betrayal: Bruno is betrayed by his parents, Hilary by her parents, Joshua by his clients, the sheriff by his deputy, and even Bruno's psychiatrist violates the trust between patient and doctor. Did you plan this when you started the novel, or did it just naturally evolve?

KOONTZ: My childhood was a nightmare. I referred to my father earlier. He held forty jobs in thirty-four years—and managed to be unemployed during some big chunks of time. He was an alcoholic who was always winding up in bar fights. The violent streak in him was evident even when he had not been drinking, and when drunk he could be a terror. He made my life and that of my mother a living hell, and I was never happier than when he periodically took up with another woman and stayed away from home for a few days—or even for just one night, because that meant a night of peace. I loved my mother deeply, and it was her love for me—a splendid and selfless and deep commitment—that brought me through my childhood in relatively good psychological condition. If she had just been able to understand my love of books and could have encouraged me in that instead of coming down foursquare against the whole thing, I might've gotten out of adolescence entirely unscarred. On the other hand, I'll never be able to understand why she stayed with my father in spite of all that he did to her and me. It wasn't that he supported us so well, which he did not; we were damn poor, always worried about where next week's food money would come from. And it wasn't his love and affection, for he seldom exhibited any—and never any that seemed genuine. She should have walked and taken me with her, but she endured. Perhaps out of a misguided abhorrence of divorce, perhaps because in some strange way she *needed* the abuse, which is something I don't want to believe or even think about, because it makes me so sad and, sometimes, a little ill just to contemplate it. Anyway, throughout my childhood and adolescence, I saw my own father betray me and my mother in all the most fundamental ways, again and again, times without number, and that is why *Whispers* deals with children betrayed by their parents and with betrayal in general. You see, I cannot *understand* betrayal, because the most important thing we have on this earth is a handful of close relationships from which we draw the strength to go forward in adversity. Those relationships are based on trust, on mutual respect and concern and affection, and we all *need* them so desperately, and if we betray those who love us we damage no one more terribly than we damage ourselves. Betrayal of trust is stupid, emotionally suicidal, yet some people do it all the time, as a matter of course. And somehow the strongest of us are made stronger by being betrayed, and we go on—like Hilary in *Whispers*. And those who can't handle it are sometimes transformed into men like Bruno Frye. How could a writer *not* be fascinated by that theme?

MUNSTER: Would you tell us some writers you admire in the horror field?

KOONTZ: Richard Matheson has done some fine, fine work. *I Am Legend* is, to my mind, the second-best vampire story of all time, second only to *Dracula*. *The Incredible Shrinking Man* is a *tour de force*, and *Hell House* is dynamite. In his weird mood—as opposed to his SF mood—Theodore Sturgeon was untouchable; I'm thinking of great stories like "It" and "The Professor's Teddy Bear" and *Some of Your Blood*, which is one of the scariest novels I've ever read. Ira Levin's *Rosemary's Baby* is one of the few genuine classics of modern horror, a book that will live forever, as is King's *The Shining*. There are other King books of which I'm enormously fond—*Firestarter*, *The Dead Zone*, *Pet Sematary*, and to a lesser degree, *'Salem's Lot*. I think Paul Wilson is good, and I wish he'd write more than he does, and Charles Grant is always very stylish.

MUNSTER: When not writing, what type of stories do you read?

KOONTZ: I read everything: John D. MacDonald is a great hero of mine, Elmore Leonard, Ross Thomas, William Goldman, the above-mentioned horror writers and others in the genre, Herman Wouk, Dickens, Raymond Chandler, Jack Vance, Jim Harrison, Mary Higgins Clark, Dick Francis, Gore Vidal, Roger Zelazny, Ed McBain and Evan Hunter, William F. Buckley, scores of others, and about a hundred magazines ranging from science journals to *Fortune*, from *National Review* on the right to *New Republic* on the left. People seem to like the bizarrely twisted plots and exotic information in my books, and I'm convinced that if I didn't keep cramming my head full of stuff, from a thousand sources, I'd produce less interesting novels. Television, by the way, is the death of creativity, and any writer who spends much time at all in front of the idiot box is going to mummify his own imagination and wind up producing dusty, dessicated, empty books.

MUNSTER: In your novel, *The Voice of the Night*, Roy Borden wants to kill someone and rape someone. Several years ago I had a student who wanted, in the worst way, to kill someone at point blank range to see what it would look like. He also wrote in his journal that he wanted to rape one of the teachers in my school. Is Roy Borden modeled after anybody?

KOONTZ: Roy Borden—and here's another case of a kid gone wrong due to the pressures of a horrible childhood—is modeled on that type of sly bully we have all known as kids, the one who relies less on physical intimidation and more on psychological pressure and the force of his personality to instigate mischief (even evil) and to draw others into his schemes.

MUNSTER: *Darkfall* would lend itself nicely to being on the screen. Would you want to write the screenplay, and if so, would there be any part you'd leave out or add?

KOONTZ: There was a lot of interest in the film rights to *Darkfall* when it was first put on the market. But that was several months before the release of *Gremlins*, and a lot of people seemed to think it might be too similar. Of course, there turned out to be no similarity at all—except for the small threatening creatures—but Hollywood's thinking patterns are not always logical or rational. I have done some screen work—two different scripts of *The Face of Fear* for two different producers, an episode of the old NBC series *CHiPs*, and some other stuff—and I would not be adverse to doing a screenplay from one of my own books if the offer came along. But I have turned down film work on occasion because, at the moment, I think of myself as a Book Person rather than a Film Person. I rather dislike the necessary collaboration of the film medium. A book is mine, and no one else's, and I bear the credit or blame for every word and comma. But a film is so collaborative that no one person can honestly claim the majority of credit or blame, and the ego is not put on the line in the same way as it is when one writes a book. Therefore, it is easier, in film, not to demand the best of oneself. Books are more challenging, riskier, and therefore more fulfilling.

MUNSTER: Land of Enchantment has published a special edition of your book, *Twilight Eyes*. Would you explain how this came about?

KOONTZ: Chris Zavisa, who *is* Land of Enchantment, came to me after he'd done *The Cycle of the Werewolf*, and said, "How about doing a story for me that I could publish in similar fashion, with lots of color and black-and-white illustrations?" I had bought the super-limited $200 edition of *Cycle of the Werewolf* and had felt I'd gotten my money's worth (incredibly!), so I was delighted to work with him. He said he wanted something longer than King's piece, which was essentially a long short story or short novelette. He asked for a 25,000-word novella. I agreed and set to work. But I became so thoroughly captivated by the story, background, and characters of *Twilight Eyes* that I ended up with an entire novel of 125,000 words, five times what he wanted! Poor Chris aged a year during the minute it took him to open the manuscript box, check the length, and calculate the horrendous run-up in publishing costs. But he liked it a lot, and he is too much of a gentleman to convey in words the curses he must have been mentally heaping upon my head. Phil Parks has spent a year doing the artwork, which is truly spectacular, and even if I weren't involved in the project I would say this is going to be the most beautifully and generously illustrated novel anyone has ever seen. Phil has done absolutely *gorgeous* work in this, and more than a few of the pieces actually brought a chill of horror to me when I saw them. Chris has published it in a limited and signed edition; the first 50 include an original drawing by Phil Parks tipped in, and sell for $250, and the next 200 are signed and numbered but without a drawing at $75, and then there'll be an unsigned trade edition of 5,000 at a lower price, and Chris has been so lavish in use of color and in design points that I think he'll probably break even on the project. I admire his gutsiness and his determination not to compromise quality, and I sure hope he'll make enough off a trade paperback some day and off participation in other editions to make it worth his while. (But hey, Chris, if you lose the house over this, sorry, but you *can't* move into our garage!).

MUNSTER: Peter Straub and Stephen King teamed up with *The Talisman*. Is there any author you'd like to team up with on a novel?

KOONTZ: I think collaborations are seldom successful. Collaborative books are usually less interesting than the books that the writers would have produced working alone. King and Straub may be an exception, but to be absolutely sure of that, I'd have to see another book or two by them. A definite exception to that rule is the work done by Larry Niven and Jerry Pournelle. *Lucifer's Hammer* was an absolute roller-coaster ride, and *Inferno* was a pure delight, *The Mote in God's Eye* was damn good, too, and I am about to read *Footfall*, which I hear is first-rate. As good as they are separately, they seem even better in tandem, and *that* is a rare thing. Collaboration is not for me. I tried it once and did not like it much. I'm so damn sure I know what's *right* in a story that I become a bastard about concessions, alterations, and compromises. If I were to be forced to work in collaboration very much, I would wind up as a headline in the *National Enquirer*: KOONTZ KILLS COLLABORATOR WITH CUISINART OVER DISPUTE ABOUT SEMICOLON. In my heart, I am still a little boy, writing stories on tablet paper, binding them with tape, and they're all mine, mine, *mine.*

MUNSTER: David Axton, Brian Coffey, K. R. Dwyer, Leigh Nichols, Anthony North, Richard Paige, Owen West, and John Hill are some of the pseudonyms that you've used. Is there any significance to any of these names?

KOONTZ: None whatsoever. I looked for short, punchy names in some cases—Owen West, John Hill. In other cases the idea was to find a name that fell pleasantly on the ear—Anthony North, Leigh Nichols. In the case of Brian Coffey, I wanted a name that was Scottish because I'd noted that many writers of thrillers had Scottish names—MacLean, Innes, etc.—so Coffey was first Brian Mac-something, MacFudd, I don't know what anymore, but the editor didn't like that and somehow we got around to Coffey.

MUNSTER: Both *Watchers* and *Shadowfires* deal in molecular nightmares. Did it concern you as you wrote these novels that there was a similarity in the themes?

KOONTZ: Nope. Genetic engineering is such a fascinating subject that I could write twenty novels on the subject without any of those books being repetitive. In fact, I've got several very strong ideas for books using the subject, but I won't be writing them any time soon, partly because some time needs to pass between the recent books and anything else on the subject, and partly because I've got other ideas that I like even better.

MUNSTER: Many of your earlier stories had poetic titles such as *The Fall of the Dream Machine*, *A Darkness in My Soul*, and "Soft Come the Dragons." When you moved into your suspense fiction the titles became shorter—*Watchers*, *Strangers*, and *Darkfall*. Why the brevity in titles?

KOONTZ: Publishers' expectations, in part. They like shorter titles, especially for suspense. I've used a few longer ones, of course: *The Face of Fear*, *Twilight Eyes*; and three of the Nichols books, *The Key to Midnight*, *The Eyes of Darkness*, *The House of Thunder*. Now *there* was a pattern that I couldn't have kept up for long: Pocket Books expected all the Nichols titles to have the same four-word pattern, the same rhythm, *and* to embody an image of something that did not in fact exist—*i.e.*, there is no key to midnight, the darkness has no eyes, and a house cannot be built of thunder. I told my editor that if we kept that pattern for very long, I'd be reduced to a title like *The Lips of Sofas*. Anyway, there are likely to be some future books that break the one-word pattern I've had lately. It's only partly a calculated thing to use one word; after all, the single word is often the best title by far. The title for *Strangers* comes from a multitude of uses of the word in complex ways throughout the story, and no other title would sum it up nearly as well, or, in such a neat way, be an antonym for the book's theme of family. *Whispers* could have no better title, for the same reason: it ties in repeatedly and intimately with the thematic structure of the novel. Likewise *Lightning*, on which I'm now at work.

MUNSTER: You're emphatic about not being called a horror writer, when in fact some of your stories (*Phantoms*, *Twilight Eyes*, "Hardshell," and "Snatchers" to name a few) all seem to be horror stories. How do you define horror, and why are you so adamant about not being called a horror writer?

KOONTZ: First of all, I am not a horror novelist. I intend to continue writing short pieces like "The Black Pumpkin" or "Down in the Darkness" or the stories for *Night Visions 4*, that are unquestionably in the genre. So I am a horror writer to some extent, but not in my longer work, at least not any more, and not to the exclusion of other types of fiction. I believe my only real horror novels are *Darkfall*, *The Funhouse*, *The Mask*, and maybe *The Vision* and *Phantoms*. The first three, you will note, are the only novels I've ever written that contain elements of the supernatural, and I believe to qualify as horror a novel must have some small element, at least, of the supernatural. Granted, in *The Vision* my lead character is a psychic. But she is not in tune with the dead, does not conduct séances, that sort of thing. Her psychic ability is narrow, clearly defined, and almost scientific in its nature, totally detached from any connection with the occult world. Although *Phantoms* has a monster—and I like to think a real creepy one—I just don't think of it as horror because *there is a well-reasoned, logical, scientific explanation* for the monster's existence—and almost as important as that is the fact the characters in the story do not resort to religion or to superstition or occult devices to defeat the beast, but they destroy it by the application of logic, reason, and modern technology. I think *Phantoms* is a mainstream novel with a large measure of suspense, a large though somewhat smaller measure of science fiction, and still smaller measure of horror *effects*. The same thing can be said of *Twilight Eyes*; it has its monsters, but their source is ultimately understandable, logical; they are not ghosts, demons. As for why I don't want to have the label "horror writer...." Well, I work very hard to write novels that bridge genres, have a mainstream sensibility, and attempt to portray the broad spectrum of human emotions and relationships. But when I'm stuck with a label, a lot of people who would enjoy my books will never read them because they will think the label actually defines what I do; yet what I do is much broader than just horror. I love good horror fiction, but I'd be creatively smothered if I tried to spend the rest of my life writing to genre expectations. And by the way of additional explanation, let me tell you what I said in a recent interview in *The Horror Show*: too many writers in the field are content to go for the jugular, give their readers a chill—and that's it. Boring. They don't seek to explore other emotions, the whole complex web of human thought and feeling, and as a result the genre has gotten a reputation of being stale, one-note fiction. I am just not pleased to have my work lumped with the majority of what bears the horror label these days, primarily because too much horror is strictly negativistic, misanthropic, and therefore drearily predictable. You can't find much hope, love, or optimism in current horror, but you can find all the nihilism you want, enough doom-saying and cynicism and pessimism—a sort of self-conscious "hipness" that is based on the juvenile notion that optimists are squares. You see, by accepting the label, I have to accept all of the associations that come with it, and damned if I'll do that.

MUNSTER: Then how would you describe yourself as a writer? What label *does* fit?

KOONTZ: I am a novelist of the fantastic who writes in a realistic vein. In *Strangers*, for instance, the world of the story is demonstrably our world, with a cast of characters from every region of the country, in a variety of occupations, and through them we have a fairly detailed picture of the *real* world in which we live, not a world where demons or haunted houses or vampires are possible, but a world in which the *fantastic* exists to the extent that it does in real life: the existence of aliens in the universe is no more proven than the existence of demons, but logic tells us that the existence of aliens is a very real possibility while the existence of demons is unlikely in the extreme. The dog and The Outsider in *Watchers* are fantastic creatures, but their creation is shown to be a logical development based on current or near-future human knowledge, not magical or occult in any way. Horror novelists deal with human fears by exaggerating them and embodying them in symbolic figures like vampires and werewolves and ghosts. On the other hand, when I write about human fears, I write about the actual fears themselves—the fear of losing a loved one, the fear of failure, the fear of being alone—and the elements of the fantastic are not devices by which I obscure the nature of the *real* fears of which I'm writing—as are vampires, for instance—but serve as lenses by which I can more closely examine what those real fears are.

A Dean Koontz Interview, by Bill Munster

MUNSTER: "Twilight of the Dawn" is by far your most emotional story. It would almost seem terribly contrived of me to call it stunning, but that's exactly what it was. After writing a story of this caliber, what do you do to come down? Was this story at all biographical?

KOONTZ: When you get hold of a story like "Twilight of the Dawn," you're very high, really flying, because you're always aware of the real stuff, the good stuff, when you get your hands on it. You say to yourself, "Good God, look at what I've stumbled onto here! This is elemental, profound, and it fell to me to write it!" And when you're working at that level...it's funny, but that's when you don't have to struggle with the language to make it shine or strain to keep the thematic structure tight. It just *flows*. You are at those moments in touch with something in yourself that is almost primal, instinctual, yet something that finds natural expression through the use of language. It's weird. And wonderful.

MUNSTER: Your short short, "Hardshell" is clearly a spinoff (the alien beast among us) of *Twilight Eyes*. Is there any chance that you'll tap some of the characters and situations in *Phantoms*?

KOONTZ: Nope.

MUNSTER: You sold the film rights of *Phantoms* to Dino DeLaurentiis, and the rights to *Watchers* to Roger Corman. Will you be having any input to the movies?

KOONTZ: Very little. Movie folk like to forget that there was a novel in the first place, because then they can think of the project as having evolved from their own inspiration. With this attitude, they find the novelist an unhappy reminder that the project did not spring full-blown from their own mighty brains.

MUNSTER: "Down in the Darkness," "Black Pumpkin," and "Snatchers" all share a common seed—an intense richness of prose when describing the darkness. In "Down in the Darkness" the blackness of a cellar is described as "...a black mass that seemed to throb in expectation of my final advance into its embrace"; in "Snatchers," you write that Billy Meeks won't venture out "into the frigid darkness"; and in "The Black Pumpkin," Toomy resolves to "cloak himself in darkness." Without even mentioning your novels (in *Strangers*, for instance, Ernie Block is petrified of the darkness), how are you able to come up with so many similes and metaphors for the dark? Does this come naturally, or do you find yourself having to think about each for awhile?

KOONTZ: Finding new images, new ways to use words, not just to describe darkness but to describe anything about which one writes, is challenging. For me, images must not only be vivid but apt, and they must be in harmony with the music of the line in which they appear. Prose *has* music, you know. There is a melody and rhythm to each sentence, a stronger melody and rhythm to each paragraph, and stronger still in each scene. Michael R. Collings once told me he found *Twilight Eyes* to be written in prose that, by its rhythms, was perilously close to poetry. That was intentional. I pulled out all of the stylistic stops in that one and allowed the reader—if he was perceptive—to *hear* the music of prose at full volume. But I am always aware of the potential music in any story I write, in the musical *flow* of the words—sometimes its light music, sometimes dark, sometimes humorous, music of a thousand different styles and moods—and I work hard to give the sentences and paragraphs the right underlying music to support the obvious mood I'm seeking to convey on the surface. Sometimes editors can't understand why, when they suggest that we cut a sentence, I have to rework the sentences all around the cut. I don't rework them for surface meaning, you understand. But when one sentence is cut for whatever reason, the underlying music of the paragraph is altered, and rewriting is required on *that* level, beneath the surface, to restore that music. I've met very few writers who think of prose this way, who see the hidden rhythms in good writing, the melodies, and those who do have the insight are usually among my personal favorites. Anyway, my reviews often say that my prose is super-smooth, that it goes down as easy as apple juice, or that it is "transparent" and therefore easy to read; but in fact the style is far from transparent; I believe that what they're all perceiving and floundering to explain is the way my writing—at least when it's at its best—flows with a musical kind of energy. When it's at its worst...well, it's like a dog trying to sing the entire score of *Turandot*. The poor mutt *wants* to do well, but he isn't equipped to perform the piece.

MUNSTER: In everything you write there is one common thread: that the human spirit is unstoppable and good. Is this just a philosophy you employ in fiction, or do you believe it yourself?

KOONTZ: I am a raving optimist. There are those among us who are vile and wicked, yes, but they're the genetic freaks, the failures in the species. I think for the most part that the human species is indeed a reflection of something godlike and that within us is the potential for wonders. I like people.

MUNSTER: A very distinct characteristic of a Koontz novel is the use of dialogue to move a story along. You can go several pages of nothing but dialogue and never lose a reader. With this penchant for capturing dialogue, would you ever want to write a screenplay or stage production?

KOONTZ: I have written screenplays somewhat successfully, though I've never spent much time at it. I intend to do more scripts on spec in the years ahead. But my first love is the novel and always will be. Just yesterday, I was working on a scene in *Lightning*, and the dialogue was some of the best I've ever written. One of the characters is a clever, mordant woman, and some of what she was saying had me laughing aloud. I think dialogue is equal to action as the best tool with which to explore character and reveal it.

MUNSTER: The richness of characters in *Strangers* comes close to being a tribute to Charles Dickens. Were you doing this intentionally, or did the story idea warrant a greater understanding of the characters?

KOONTZ: A number of reviews of both *Strangers* and *Watchers* called those books "Dickensian," and I suppose that in part what they were referring to were the number of the characters and their colorfulness. I love Dickens's work and have talked about that in other interviews, so it'd be a surprise if some of my fondness for Dickens didn't show up in my own work. And I suspect what makes people think of the comparison is also the view of people that I seem to share with Dickens. He was a people lover and a shameless optimist. My God, even when he wrote about the French Revolution in *A Tale of Two Cities*, when he dwelt on the blood and horror, when he explored with despair the fact that radical political solutions only lead to oppression by one side or the other; and though he pulled no punches in depicting people's willingness to participate in atrocities for a noble cause, he kept his faith in the individual, in the beauty and power of friendship and kinship. *A Tale of Two Cities* has what is, in my opinion, the most powerful final scene of any novel in the English language. When that poor, damned, alcoholic attorney proves his love by going to the guillotine in the place of his loved one's *fiancé*, and when on the way to the blade he finds the additional strength to be a witness for and to give courage to a young woman who is also to be executed unjustly, he is a symbol of the moral superiority of the individual—even a badly flawed individual—over the state; and in his sacrifice there is a sense of the transcendence of the human spirit that is so wonderfully moving and true. If I could ever write a scene of that power, that complexity, that profoundity.... The hope of doing so is what keeps me going, day to day.

MUNSTER: Finally, what are some of the future writing projects you have going?

KOONTZ: I'm finishing *Lightning* now. Other than that.... There are several books in the planning stages, but I won't talk about them. I loathe talking about works in progress, and even my publishers don't know what a book's about until the finished script is in their hands.

IV.

DEAN KOONTZ AND STEPHEN KING:

STYLE, *INVASION*, AND AN AESTHETICS OF HORROR

BY MICHAEL R. COLLINGS

When asked to write *Stephen King as Richard Bachman* in March, 1985, I quickly discovered that interest in King's pseudonyms outstripped information available. Within a week of King's acknowledging the Bachman pen name, several sources—publishers, book dealers, readers, and fans—had mentioned a number of possible other pseudonyms; obviously, if King admitted to two pen names, John Swithen and Richard Bachman, there might be others. The resulting pseudonym mania created a number of embarrassing developments, including the hoax-review linking King with a spurious soft-porn novel. Nor has the controversy abated significantly. Many readers still doubt King's statements that there are no other pseudonyms. I recently received a letter, for example, speculating that Michael Kimball, author of *Firewater Pond*, might be an alter ego for King. After all, no one admits to having ever met Kimball, he is supposed to be a neighbor of King's, and King was instrumental in bringing the book to the publisher's attention. Of the many rumors, however, only a few survived scrutiny. One had King as the author of *Exorcism* by "Eth Natas"; even a cursory reading of a few pages dispelled any possibility that such was the case. Others had King writing a series of westerns, a series of science-fiction novels, a novel so bad that DAW rejected it, and so forth. *Stephen King as Richard Bachman* assesses many of these rumors, rejecting most on stylistic grounds or on the basis of information King provided about his early career in "Why I Was Bachman," included in *The Bachman Books*. Most of the rumors, in fact, could have been generated by bits and pieces about the Bachman novels or by such difficult-to-locate short stories as "Slade," a parody-western published in King's college newspaper. It wouldn't take much—given the active rumor mill—for a reference to "that Western" to become inflated into a mythical series of novels. King's prolific output as a writer would only add fuel to such rumors.

Of the multiple possibilities, only one seemed a probability: *Invasion* by "Aaron Wolfe." Shortly after beginning *Stephen King as Richard Bachman*, I read the novel. It seems likely, on the basis of textual similarities, that King could have written the novel. Setting, characters, plot lines, images, prose style—all corresponded to what readers have come to expect from King. I sent copies to other readers; their responses ranged from "perhaps" to "without a doubt"—King was the author.

Working independently through the question, Don Herron refers in "The Biggest Horror Fan of Them All" to what he considered King's "next published novel" after *Carrie*, a work that "might also pass as the work of a writer struggling to make it into professional print, and hitting on horror-science fiction as a possible market": Wolfe's *Invasion*. Herron points to correspondences in plot as well *as* stylistic divergences between the novel and *The Shining*, for example, but concludes that "surely it is King writing for the rigid formula demanded by the publishers." (39)

Even before I completed the first draft of *Stephen King as Richard Bachman*, however, Rob Reginald of Borgo Press assured me that King *did not* write *Invasion*. He knew the author and had seen a copy of the novel on the author's shelf in the author's home.

And the author was Dean Koontz.

Reginald asked that I not publicize Koontz as author, even though Borgo Press's *Guide to SF in LC Classification* had already explicitly identified "Wolfe" as Koontz. As a result, the conclusion of the "Speculations" chapter in *Stephen King as Richard Bachman* links *Invasion* to "one of King's contemporaries" without specifying which one.

Since *Stephen King as Richard Bachman* appeared, however, it has become common knowledge that Koontz wrote *Invasion*—much to the dismay of dealers who stockpiled copies on the chance that it was by King. If paperback first editions of the Bachman novels brought prices up to $140 each, surely *Invasion*, should it turn out to be by King, would do the same. But it was by Koontz and therefore no longer in the sweepstakes as a King collectible; ironically, with Koontz's recent successes with *Twilight Eyes* and *Strangers* (which reached the *New York Times* Bestseller's List) and his subsequent two-novel contract, copies of *Invasion* may again become more valuable as Koontz collectibles. Already several dealers in the Southern California area near my home have reported an upsurge in requests for Koontz material.

The identification of "Aaron Wolfe," however, did not resolve what seemed the most interesting point of all. Even now, knowing its author, I see suggestions of King throughout *Invasion*, strong enough suggestions to give the rumor of King's authorship such persistence that it was still around a decade after the book first appeared. However incorrectly, the novel has been linked with two of the leading writers of dark fantasy, and as such provides insights into the nature of the form itself; at the same time, it allows contemporary readers an opportunity to assess the narrative devices employed by both King and Koontz.

Nothing points obviously to King in the opening lines of the text. The novel is restrained, the sentences long and carefully structured, reflecting the rational, objective first-person narrator Koontz had already explored in *Anti-Man* (1970) and *A Werewolf Among Us* (1973), quite unlike King's usual third-person narration. Yet within the first several pages, there are some intriguing details.

Invasion recounts an alien attack on an isolated farmhouse near Bangor, Maine. Herron argues that except for King, "no one else in the history of literature would have characters listening to a radio station out of Bangor" (30), although two years later (well before King and his techniques became "brand names" in horror), Koontz did indeed refer to Bangor in *Night Chills* (1976).

Invasion also suggests several of King's characters. Early in *Invasion*, Don Hanlon described his wife, Connie, as just passed thirty but still able to pass for a teenager, just as Wendy Torrance looks "very young, like a girl just getting ready to graduate from high school" (*Shining*, 60). And in *Thinner*, Bill Halleck remembers a traveling salesman mistaking his wife for a teenager (*Thinner*, 4).

In addition, Hanlon dreams, just as Billy Halleck dreams, Ray Garraty dreams, Barton George Dawes dreams, and Danny Torrance dreams—and Koontz's Baker St. Cyr and other characters dream. In each instance, the dreams focus on death and decay. Hanlon dreams of Vietnam, of being pinned down by a body until he wishes only to die. The dreams in both King and Koontz share a peculiar similarity of texture—they are clearly critical to understanding the authors' larger purposes, while simultaneously impelling the surface narrative further.

Even an image as commonplace as berries seems to connect *Invasion* to King. Toby Hanlon's pony is named Blueberry. Blueberries and strawberries occur frequently in King's fictions—"Strawberry Spring," "Children of the Corn," and "I Know What You Need" among the short stories; the strawberry juice "fresh as arterial blood" in *The Talisman* (95); *Thinner*'s sinister strawberry pie; the "splash of blueberry drool" that results from Carrie's telekinesis (7); the seductively homey "strawberry tart or blueberry buckle" in *Roadwork* (26); the single blueberry in the puzzle in *Rage* (117). The point is not, however, that they occur—after all, anyone can mention strawberries or blueberries, although they do occur far less frequently in Koontz's work than in King's. In King, though, the berries function ambiguously to suggest warm domesticity and to become vehicles for isolation and terror. "Strawberry Spring" counterpoints violent death. The soda and pie in "I Know What You Need" and "Children of the Corn" become images of a hidden horror. Halleck's pie carries the curse he intends to transfer to his wife. Carla Ordner's blueberry buckle helps Steve Ordner manipulate truth and integrity. The blueberry puzzle, the last berry in the field, emphasizes Decker's mother's disengagement from normal affections. And Toby Hanlon's pony Blueberry is not only an image of pleasure, but one of horror—her yellow-stained bones first trigger Hanlon's irrational fear of the creatures.

Or, to take another recurrent image that invites a connection with King, *Invasion* emphasizes the visual impact of the alien's eyes. For most of the novel, we do not actually see the aliens, only reflections from their eyes—huge amber eyes, saucer-shaped, glowing through the Maine darkness. One of Koontz's mutants in *Nightmare Journey* (1975), Belmondo, is "saucer-eyed," but when we look at King's fiction, we see the image used far more extensively. In *Carrie*, Billy Nolan and his friends pass three joints that glow like "the lambent eyes of some rotating Cerberus" (89). Later, cigarettes wink like demons' eyes (104). Margaret White's grandmother's eyes glowed with a "kind of witch's light" when the Devil's power was on her (120). Images in "Mrs. Todd's Shortcut" seem even more closely related to *Invasion*. Mrs. Todd has "brown eyes just like lamps" (181) and a forehead that shone like a lamp (188); one of the creatures she kills had "big yellowy eyes" (187), an accurate description of the aliens in *Invasion*. A similar emphasis on eyes occurs in "I Know What You Need," with its "red hurricane-lamp eyes" (233); in the "something green with terrible red eyes the size of footballs" in "Children of the Corn" (276); in "eyes huge and red, like spirit lamps" in "Big Wheels" (188); or in eyes "like lanterns being waved aimlessly in the dark" in "The Raft" (38-39). In King, eyes are frequently large, saucer-shaped, flaring red or yellow-like lamps—just as they are in *Invasion*. To be fair, it should also be noted that a different image is almost exclusively Koontz's. The only suggestion of the alien vessel we receive in the novel is a purple glow in the forest; in Koontz, shadows (especially those enfolding the unknown) are almost always described as purple rather than black or deep blue.

The family—the Hanlons—fits more neatly into King's categories than Koontz's. There are only three members: father, mother, one child. In King's fiction, few families extend beyond this minimum. In all five Bachman novels, for examples, the central characters come from limited families. Charlie Decker has no brothers or sisters. Ray Garraty has only a mother, overbearing and ineffectual; his father was "squaded" years before. Bart Dawes's only son died of a brain tumor, leaving just him and his wife. Ben Richards runs to insure a future for his wife and daughter. And Billy Halleck's wife and daughter eventually join him in the gypsy's curse. *Carrie*, *'Salem's Lot* (considering Ben Meats and Mark Petrie as in some sense a "family"), *The Stand*, *Firestarter*, *Cujo*, *The Dead Zone*, *Christine*, *Pet Sematary*, *The Talisman*, "The Mist"—in each, we find the same pattern. Where there are other brothers or sisters, as in "The Body," "The Word Processor of the Gods," or "Gramma," they are threats. The pattern in *Invasion* fits precisely: father, mother, single child who becomes the focus of threat or danger. Many of Koontz's novels, on the other hand, work outside of this basic triune pattern; single individuals, siblings, even twins in *Whispers*. Parents occur frequently as horrible memories rather than real presences. If King concentrates on the nuclear family, Koontz concentrates on the disintegrated family, divided beyond any hope of reconciliation. There is generally less a sense of the minimal family as focus in Koontz than in King: in *Twilight Eyes*, for example, families are infiltrated by murderous aliens; in *Strangers*, the most important relationships develop among individuals regardless of family ties.

The family's name, of course, has become even more suggestive with the publication of *IT*. In his hand-written annotations to an early version of this essay, King noted in the margin next to the preceding paragraph, "Here's a coincidence booksellers with their eyes on the buck will relish: Mike Hanlon in *IT*." Although it is certainly possible to argue that Hanlon's name could be a variation on Hatlen (the name of King's professor at UMO), the identity between the names in *Invasion* and *IT* is startling.

Another element that might suggest King is the presence of brand names. Open almost any King narrative at random, and chances are that he has included specific brand names somewhere on the page. Certainly his use of such names in *Thinner* led many readers to suspect his hand in it. *Invasion* is more restrained. Occasionally the novel refers to specific brands, but the reference to Wild Turkey bourbon (185) connects more closely to Koontz than to King, since that is Koontz's chosen brand in a number of his novels.

To this point, while there are touches to suggest King in *Invasion*, there are no definite similarities; there are, however, definite differences, based in part upon the genre of *Invasion*. King has rarely written straightforward science fiction. Except for occasional stories such as "The Star Invaders," "I Am The Doorway," "The Jaunt," or "Beachworld"—or his single novel-length science fiction narrative, *The Running Man*, and the science-fictional setting of *The Long Walk*—most of his works are dark fantasy; and even those attempts quickly shade into horror (see *Stephen King as Richard Bachman* and *The Shorter Works of Stephen King*).

Koontz, on the other hand, already had a long career in writing science fiction by the time *Invasion* was published, beginning with *Star Quest* in 1968. In fact, *Invasion* dates from the period of his decision to leave straight science fiction and attempt more ambitious and complex forms; after 1975 his novels become substantially longer as they approach into contemporary horror: *Night Chills*, *The Vision*, *Whispers*, and *Strangers*.

The differences between science fiction and horror fantasy require different perspectives, purposes, structures, narrative techniques, and vocabulary; H. P. Lovecraft's stories *sound* horrifying, just as Robert Forward's *Dragon's Egg sounds* like science fiction. Science fiction emphasizes the technological and the scientific—in other words, the external and the objective. Horror, on the other hand, depends upon the irrational, the non-objective, and the internal. *Invasion* defines that transition in Koontz, shifting emphasis from strict science fiction to horror—and as such, it also appears to make several connections with King's work. The aliens in *Invasion* are at once effectively horrific and oddly stereotypic. During most of the novel, when the aliens are at best hazy images with large, glowing amber eyes, they create the necessary intimidation and suspense. When they finally reveal themselves, however, they seem more creatures from fifties' horror films than the science-fiction aliens Koontz produced in *Nightmare Journey* (1974).

They blend mantis and grasshopper, immense insectoids with two-foot-wide heads and two saucer-sized yellow eyes. Wolfe's "aliens" seem like nothing so much as the Hollywood-generated creatures in such films as *Them!* (1954), *The Deadly Mantis* (1957), *The Beginning of the End* (1957), or *Tarantula* (1955) that King refers to so often in *Danse Macabre*. Even more to the point, they suggest the insectoid outlines young Charlie Decker sees on the tent canvas in *Rage*, and similar images in *The Long Walk* and *Roadwork* (*Stephen King as Richard Bachman* 146).

The aliens' effect in *Invasion* resembles that of the vampire in *'Salem's Lot*. To resurrect the literary vampire is difficult, given the tremendous coverage the figure has received since Stoker's encyclopedic *Dracula* in 1897. Yet King instills new vitality into the old image, to create the first viable vampire novel since *Dracula*. Koontz's resurrection of the fifties insect/alien/creature is on a similar order of imagination, breathing new life into an old image.

In *The Shining*, King again takes a conventional image, the "haunted house," and gives it new credibility. The Overlook Hotel is miles removed from Shirley Jackson's Hill House or Anne Rivers Siddons's *The House Next Door*, both physically and psychically. It attains a malevolence and sentience that sets it apart from the stereotypically horrific. In final effect, the "aliens" of *Invasion* relate more to this sort of horrific element than to the science-fictional Gott or Klaatu, Michael Rennie's alien in *The Day the Earth Stood Still* (1951).

The aliens are, however, less central to *Invasion* than is another "character," one more consistently related to horror than to science fiction—death. Chapter 12 begins and ends by specifically evoking death in images reminiscent of traditional horror novels: "The gigantic face of Death lay beneath me, the obscene mouth opened wide: and I balanced precariously—in the style of bespectacled Harold Lloyd, but grimly, grimly—on the dark and rotting lips" (121; see also 115). Here we find a number of techniques that parallel King's fiction: "dark and rotting lips" demonstrate horror rather than assert it (and coincidentally suggesting the opening of *Thinner*); the dark humor in the reference to Harold Lloyd, virtually a "brand name" for precarious humor as well as a reference to film; and overriding all, the face of death. In Hanlon's obsession with death, in his continual re-living of a life-in-death in Vietnam (an important motif, by the way, in Koontz's *After the Last Race* [1974]), in the episodes of *Invasion* themselves, we repeatedly confront the reality of death. The aliens seem almost accidental, introduced as one means of initiating an increasingly inevitable confrontation with death. From the first image of death in the yellow-stained bones of Toby's pony, Blueberry, lying on bloodless snow, the novel concentrates on death as its theme, rather than on the alien invasion of Earth.

In addition, the plot counters that of much science fiction, even much "alien invasion" science fiction. In this instance, the momentum is localized, almost private. There are only three characters, discounting the horses and the aliens themselves. No other living beings appear; we see only fleshless skeletons or crushed, bleeding bodies. Science fiction is generally a literature of more universal focus; the castastrophe is commonly widespread, effecting species, planets, and systems, as in *Warlock*, Koontz's 1972 science-fiction novel.

In *Invasion*, however, we have a narrow, almost intimate setting, more appropriate to horror fantasy. In *'Salem's Lot*, for example, the town is ultimately peopled by vampires, but except for fragmentary glimpses, we concentrate only on a handful of characters; in *The Shining*, the situation is even more restricted: Jack, Wendy, and Danny Torrance and the Overlook Hotel, with a final appearance by Dick Hallorann. Other characters appear in the novel, of course, but the horror centers on these four. In Koontz's works, the same technique appears: restricted characters and settings in novels such as *Night Chills*, *Shattered* (as K. R. Dwyer), or *The Voice of the Night* (as Brian Coffey). To this extent, *Invasion* seems more closely allied with horror fantasy than with science fiction, in spite of the presence of insectoid aliens.

The ending of the novel supports this reading. The back cover of *Invasion* quotes Philip Pollock's comment that the novel is "quite genuinely spine-chilling, well written...with a twist to the ending which I like very much." Ignoring for the moment the reference to "spine chilling," a term more appropriate perhaps to mystery, suspense, or horror than science fiction, we can note his reference to a "twist." The inversion in the final chapters, while superficially related to science fiction, again underscores the sense of horror. The aliens simply depart, without explanation or justification. In the "Epilogue," Hanlon confronts two creatures, one of them speaking through Toby. Hanlon asks them about their actions; to each question, they respond that he would not understand their actions or motives. They have read his manuscript recounting the entire experience; he would not understand what they have learned from it. They killed Mr. and Mrs. Johnson, the Hanlons' nearest neighbors; Hanlon does not understand why. He accuses the aliens of trying to absolve their guilt; they do not understand the concept. They killed animals, stripping the flesh cleanly from the bones; he could not understand why they did it. They, on the other hand, cannot understand his "bizarre behavior," behavior the reader might find eminently logical. The aliens simply announce: "We will leave this world within the hour. We have no desire to learn more of your culture, real or just contrived, whichever it may be" (189).

The novel is classified as "science fiction," but the technologies involved remain unexplained. Instead, the aliens assert that Hanlon (and by extension, the readers) would not understand, then pack up and leave. The technique is reminiscent of C. S. Lewis's *Out of the Silent Planet*. Ransom, having been kidnapped and carried on board a spacecraft heading for Mars/Malacandra, asks Weston, his captor, about the ship's propulsion. Weston refuses to define it, saying that to attempt to do so would waste time, since not five men in the world have the mathematics to understand it. Essentially, this is C. S. Lewis saying that he doesn't care how the ship reaches Mars; he refuses to engage in any science-fictional jargon merely for the sake of a superficial verisimilitude. Mark Hillegas and others have interpreted this passage as suggesting that Lewis was not interested at all in that facet of science in his novel—that the novel is not, in fact, science fiction, despite the presence of a spaceship and an alien world. Instead, Lewis was attempting a form of fantasy, a Cosmic Voyage, in which scientific explanation would be at best digressive.

The author of *Invasion* seems involved in a similar attempt, writing a narrative which suggests one genre on the surface, another in the subtext. There are, in fact, virtually no scientific or technological explanations in *Invasion*. Animals are stripped of flesh without any bloodletting, a motif repeated several times. Yet the aliens refuse to explain how such could occur, or why, in spite of Hanlon's direct question. Animals and humans are controlled mentally by the aliens; yet nowhere does Koontz explain, except in the most general terms, how the aliens can control animals, or even how (if alien and human are so mutually non-understandable) they form human thoughts. In a science-fiction novel, such lapses could be devastating; indeed, many science-fiction novelists would have concentrated on precisely those problems for resolution.

In a novel actually dedicated to horror, however, the lapses would not only be acceptable but virtually demanded. For horror to be effective, it must assert and demonstrate, not explain. It is one thing to discover the skeleton of a boy's riding pony in the snow, the bones stained as if the corpse had been dipped into a vat of acid, with no blood or gobbets of flesh anywhere to be seen. Such an episode could—and does—create horror. But to explain how and why insectoid aliens chose to perform that particular action would deflate the horror, substituting instead an intellectual response.

But *Invasion* does not rely on intellectual responses. It is visceral, both in the narrative itself and in its intended reaction within the reader. As such, it would relate more easily to the horror novels of Stephen King than to most science fiction. And by an odd quirk, one which added fuel to the speculation as to its authorship, it strongly suggests the two King novels that bracket it: *'Salem's Lot* and *The Shining*.

Connections with *'Salem's Lot* are minor and fairly generalized. Both novels work within the same geographic framework—an isolated section of New England. The central characters of each are writers (both King and Koontz often explore the artist—and art—as hero). Ben Mears had published two novels, *Conway's Daughter* and *Air Dance*; in the Prologue to *'Salem's Lot*, King refers to Mears's third novel, a manuscript completed after his experiences in the town. Hanlon had published one book, a diary of his experiences in Vietnam, published while he was virtually catatonic, immured in a sanitarium—a state of mind that parallels Mears's and Mark Petrie's closely. And at the end of *Invasion*, Hanlon has completed another novel, written under compulsion and designed to make the events of the novel understandable, if not to the aliens, then to Hanlon himself. "If we survive the ordeal at Timberlake Farm," he says, "I could best cleanse my soul of the stain if I put the story down on paper" (106). The implication in King's prologue—Mears is impelled to write the novel, even after his publisher rejects the initial outline—is that Mears's writing in some way fulfills a similar purpose.

The need for explanation also appears in both novels. The evil in each is specifically external; the aliens arrive from some unnamed and unknown world in a ship that is never clearly described. Twice Hanlon sees a violent purple glow in the distance; otherwise, we see nothing. Barlow similarly appears almost from nowhere, an inexplicable intrusion into reality. Yet at the same time, the external threat becomes internal as well. Both Hanlon and Mears are aware of the traditions surrounding their experiences—the expectations of science fiction and of horror as defined by films and novels. Hanlon's expectations are raised by and justified by his background as a child; he interprets the aliens' actions according to Hollywood scripts. Mears likewise falls back on literary tradition and legend in dealing with the vampire. Perhaps only because he believes wholeheartedly in those traditions, he is able to wrest a minor victory at the end of the novel, one parallelling Hanlon's (and even more clearly parallelling the conclusion to *IT*, with its emphasis on child-like belief). In Koontz's *After the Last Race*, Hollywood and the cinema play an equally critical role.

In both *Invasion* and *'Salem's Lot*, the battle narrows to three parties: the man, the boy, and the alien. In each, the woman is lost. Neighbors who should support the hero's efforts against the invading alien are either killed during the course of the narrative (or turned into vampires), or dead from the beginning. Jimmy Cody is killed by multiple stab wounds as he falls into the darkened cellar of Mrs. Miller's boarding house; and although King does not describe the actual death, leaving it to Ben Mears's later retelling for Mark Petrie, the means and resulting horrific image strongly resemble Connie Hanlon's death:

> The thing was on her in an instant, clutching her with
> its forelegs, plunging the stinger into her stomach.
> The razored tip of it came out of her back, streaming
> blood and yellow ichor. (176)

In Cody's case, the instrument is not an alien's stinger, but kitchen knives embedded in plywood—but the final result is the same, visually and effectively.

Such similarities, however, cannot disguise the essential differences between the two. *Invasion* is narrower in scope, more streamlined in narrative thrust. It involves three people, one family; a second family, the Johnsons, is already dead by the time Hanlon arrives. The only other outside contact they attempt, a telephone call, is abruptly terminated. *'Salem's Lot* is wider, encompassing an entire town. In addition, *'Salem's Lot* is far less optimistic. Ben Mears and Mark Petrie escape, to hide in Mexico until Mark recovers in part from the shock. Ben is scarred emotionally, Mark psychically, but both survive, apparently to return to *'Salem's Lot* in a sequel King has mentioned (a film, *Return to 'Salem's Lot* is reported in the September 1986 issue of *Castle Rock* as being readied for production). *Invasion* is more optimistic but equally ambiguous. Connie Hanlon is not dead...or rather, she was dead and is resurrected by the aliens' nameless technology. The aliens leave, almost without explanation; humanity wins in spite of its flaws and weaknesses. In an inversion of everything Hanlon had discovered in Vietnam, he now knows that death is not final; the universe is a madhouse,

> And we are lunatics in this madhouse, but we have
> learned to live with it—a necessity, since there is no
> hope of being released from it. As Toby and I sat on
> the edge of the bed and the three of us hugged one an-
> other, the night was filled with our maniacal but un-
> deniably happy laughter. (190)

Connections between *Invasion* and *The Shining* (1977) are more precise; *Invasion* could, in fact, stand as an early draft moving more toward science fiction than toward horror (*Stephen King as Richard Bachman*, 148-149).

Three people—father, mother, son—are isolated not only by distance (negligible in *Invasion*) but by winter storms. They have no physical means of contacting others until after their moment of crisis has passed. The fathers are debilitated. In *Invasion*, Hanlon had recently returned from a hospital after a period of war-induced catatonia. Connie and Toby must avoid references either to Vietnam or to his hospitalization; Hanlon, speaking for himself in the first-person narrative, comments on the artificial texture their fear imposes on their relationship. In *The Shining*, Jack Torrance is equally handicapped psychologically and psychically, and equally subject to implicit censure and distrust; like Hanlon, he has not yet proven the depths of his recovery. His debilitations are more internal than extremal, however, due to alcoholism and the urge to child-abuse. Because Jack's terrors are internal, writing *The Shining* became a "ritual burning" for King, a purgation that "flowed, almost whole, from my subconscious" ("On *The Shining*," 14). *The Shining* clearly reflects the fluidity of composition, its complexities handled with unusual grace and skill. *Invasion* lacks that sense. Hanlon's flaws arise largely from without and were imposed upon him. The novel, perhaps by virtue of being pseudonymous, lacks a clearly defined sense of author.

Both fathers are also writers (as was Ben Mears). Hanlon's first book reflected his experiences in Vietnam, just as Jack Torrance's abortive play reflected his internal state before coming to the Overlook. Both see their writing as therapeutic. The outcome, of course, differs for each. Torrance rejects his play and enters the mad drama of the Overlook; Hanlon completes his book and makes possible Toby's return and Connie's restoration.

There is, as well, a fundamental difference between the two fathers. In *Invasion* Hanlon misjudges his situation and loses; the aliens kill Connie and abduct Toby. But in a larger sense, he wins. He works through his obsessions to greater clarity. While the aliens apparently win, withdrawing from the Earth through their own choice, Hanlon is reunited with Toby and Connie. Jack Torrance also misjudges virtually everything around him; his misjudgments, however, result in death and destruction. The horrors within overcome him, until he joins the evil and attempts to kill his own wife and son. The Overlook wins; Wendy and Danny barely escape.

The wives, Wendy Torrance and Connie Hanlon, respond similarly to the crisis. Both have survived their husbands' withdrawal: Connie, when Hanlon returns from Vietnam catatonic; Wendy, when Jack submits to his alcoholism and his tendencies to violence. Yet both are strong, protecting their sons. In many ways, both overreact, threatening their sons' abilities to mature.

Both boys seem older than their years, a characteristic of King's fictions. Parents in both novels, in fact, remark on the strength their sons show under impossible, unimaginable situations. The plots of both *Invasion* and *The Shining* require this greater maturity. In both novels, the sons form a crux. Toby Hanlon's mind is easy to control and manipulate; therefore the aliens must have him in order to communicate with Hanlon. In the final chapter, in fact, Koontz refers to the "Toby-alien" as the two identities merge. Through Toby, acting literally as mouthpiece for the aliens, Hanlon comes to understand himself. Danny Torrance is likewise the object of attention; the Overlook wants him. Since he has "the shine," his mind is open to it, necessary to it. In both novels, the action revolves around keeping the son safe. Again, of course, there is the fundamental difference: in one, the father works for the son's welfare; in the other, against it.

The characters' deaths provide an additional connection. Connie Hanlon's is specifically graphic in a novel in which skeletons appear but actual moments (and causes) of death do not. In keeping with the fifties "creature-features" that *Invasion* so strongly resembles, the insectoid alien unsheathes a yard-long stinger—a green "chitinous saber" dripping with poison—and thrusts it through her abdomen, its tip protruding from her back. She dies; Hanlon comments that there is no doubt of it. The effect of the venom was "purely academic" (176). Yet in the final chapter, she is not dead. Mr. and Mrs. Johnson cannot be restored, but Don finds Connie sitting in their bed, as beautiful as ever. The aliens do not explain how they restored her; if Hanlon were an intelligent creature, they state, he would already know (189). Jack's "death" follows the same pattern. He attacks Wendy. She stabs him with a kitchen knife; he dies and his body is possessed by the Overlook. Only once more does "Jack" surface, when he finally confronts Danny on the third floor. Danny does not run; instead, he challenges the thing that was his father. For an instant, Jack is restored, just long enough to look at Danny and reassert his love for his son.

Science fiction into horror...if Stephen King had published *Invasion* pseudonymously, the shift from one genre to another might explain virtually all of the structural and thematic differences between *Invasion* and *The Shining*. The latter novel is certainly more complex, a greater achievement by any standard of judgment. Even in its structure, it suggests greater finesse. *Invasion* is straight-line, first-person narrative (and Koontz recently spoke of a wish to revise the book to bring it more into line with the possibilities the narrative suggests). While both novels begin in the fall and move toward the dead of winter, *Invasion* does so through the simple expedient of arranging (and identifying) chapters by days and hours, a device repeated in varying forms in Koontz's *After the Last Race*, *The Vision*, and *Darkfall*. Structure in

The Shining is more complicated, interweaving a number of simultane-
ous actions and perceptions, shifting from character to character, allowing the multiple parts to blend within the reader's mind and create
the whole. In "On *The Shining*," King refers to his original conception
of *The Shining* as a five-act Shakespearean tragedy, an idea he admits
was pretentious yet fundamental to what he hoped to achieve.

Read in the context of King's fiction, including *'Salem's Lot*
and *The Shining, Rage, The Long Walk*, and *Roadwork, Invasion* does
share a number of characteristics. None of them are definitive; there
was not enough evidence simply to assert that Stephen King wrote *Invasion*.

On the other hand, the similarities were sufficiently strong,
sufficiently intriguing to keep alive the speculation.

Much of this article may seem an exercise in futility to many
readers. After all, if we *know* that Koontz wrote the novel, why discuss
it in terms of King?

The answer is that *Invasion* may be more important than
merely a single novel involved in a controversy over authorship. Instead, it can be viewed as a kind of touchstone. If there is sufficient
internal evidence to link it to King—however inaccurately, as it turns
out—perhaps it could serve as an indicator of what both King and
Koontz are attempting in their fiction.

That is, since there is no question of Koontz "borrowing" from
King, or vice versa, it seems likely that the similarities between the two
authors stem from elements inherent within the genre itself. Brand-
name descriptions, carefully established realism of setting and character, common images, and themes may themselves become, not trademarks of a single author (as we frequently assume when we talk of
King's brand names), but characteristics of dark fantasy itself, part of
the realism of presentation that C. S. Lewis argued was essential to
fantasy at any level.

Thus a number of themes, images, and devices are shared between King and Koontz. Brand names, already mentioned briefly, play
an important part in both, although far more so in King than in Koontz.
Similarly, both writers depend heavily upon filmic imagery, to the
point that one reviewer referred to King as the "master of postliterate
prose," a negative phrase meaning that King's primary effect on readers
is to stimulate recollection of images from film and television. A similar effect occurs in Koontz's fiction, again to a lesser extent. Still, in
novels such as *After the Last Race* (1974), *The Vision* (1977), and
Whispers (1980), Koontz uses off-handed references to Rhett and Scarlet, or Dorothy and Oz, or Cary Grant in *To Catch a Thief* as means of
establishing characterization. In *After the Last Race*, a non-fantasy
thriller published the same year as *Invasion*, Lou Velinski self-con-
sciously defines himself in terms of films, while others identify their
reactions to stress as analogues to episodes of films.

Cancer plays an important role in King's prose as an image of a devastating contemporary horror. From *Roadwork* and *The Running Man* through *The Talisman* and *Thinner*, cancer recurs consistently as a thematic device—the knowable horror we all face daily. In *After the Last Race* cancer plays a pivotal role; Ely Grimes's reaction to leukemia instigates the series of events that disrupts the flawless plans for a robbery. Again, Koontz relies less heavily on cancer as symbol or image than does King; still, he acknowledges its prevalence as threat.

It is even possible to find parallels between the two writers that seem closer than commonplace image or theme. Koontz's pyromaniac in *After the Last Race* seems a tamer, rather sane version of King's Trashcan Man in *The Stand*. The Black Presence of *Nightmare Journey* (1975) parallels—to a limited extent at least—the Dark Man figure that recurs throughout King's writings, from "The Dark Man," published while he was still in college, through *The Stand*, *The Dark Tower*, and *The Eyes of the Dragon*. At the level of typography and visual arrangement of words, we notice a consistent use of italics in both writers, although King's sense of italics as interruptives is much sharper than Koontz's. Both make full use of indented, single-line intrusions in paragraphs, a technique King says he developed through reading Vonnegut's novels (see *Stephen King as Richard Bachman*, 77-78). And both explore (and exploit) to the fullest the rhythms of colloquial, contemporary speech using a style that becomes at times almost transparent—that is, the reader notices only what is said, not how it is said. In a letter dated 14 January 1986, Koontz commented on the surface similarities of their styles, then analyzed the underlying differences. King's prose is stylistically transparent because his narrative voice is familiar, "that of a favorite uncle or maybe a grandfather—albeit an uncle or grandfather with a more than usually twisted mind!" It is in fact, according to Koontz, "the author's personal voice untainted by a voice specific to character, which makes each successively even more cozy to the reader than the one before it."

In his own work, transparency results from an opposite technique:

> In my stuff, for better or worse, the voice varies more from tale to tale, and even within the same tale when the viewpoint shifts with the scene. Transparency of style must therefore be achieved neither by colloquial rhythms nor by King's subtle constant echoing of archetypal real-life storytellers (uncles and grandfathers, the Uncle Remuses of our day-to-day life). Instead, I strive (and the level of success varies) to create a character of depth and purity that, though not necessarily of a type immediately familiar to the reader from his daily life, swiftly becomes familiar in

the early chapters; then the particular character's
voice, if true, grows more transparent—and more
real—page by page.

Such a strategy requires an inordinate number of revisions—
facilitated by the word processor. In *Whispers*, for example, Koontz
averaged thirty-one reworkings per page. Such multiple revisions are
characteristic of Koontz's later prose—*Night Chills* and the novels following; *Invasion*, he notes, is not representative of his best writing, in
part because it was completed in four weeks to help Barry Malzberg
meet a commitment to Laser Books.

During the summer of 1984, I immersed myself in contemporary dark fantasy, reading most of King then available, much of
Koontz, all of Peter Straub, and a smattering of other current writers.

As I read, it was easy to notice the differences in quality between King, Koontz, and Straub, for example, and a number of less effective writers. Straub wrote on a consistently literary level, his structures often as interesting and effective as his content. King and Koontz,
on the other hand, rarely drew attention to themselves, emphasizing instead the narrative itself. In fact, in novels such as Koontz's *Whispers*
(1980), *Phantoms* (1983), and *Darkfall* (1984), I noted passages that
could easily have fit into King novels as well. Given the controversy
over the authorship of *Invasion*, coupled with the fact that in the inter-
vening decade King and Koontz have moved closer and closer in technique, content, and approach, we might not wonder at such occasional
tonal blendings.

With the publication of a major novel by both King and
Koontz within six months of each other, the underlying thrust of contemporary dark fantasy becomes even clearer. Koontz's *Strangers* and
King's *IT* (to which list one might perhaps add Straub's *Floating
Dragon*) graphically illustrate the parallels that mark these two leading
practitioners of dark fantasy. Each novel is long—the longest either has
published to date. Each incorporates complexly intertwined, multiple
narratives focusing on several characters—circling the ultimate truth the
novel intends to reveal, but never quite penetrating it until the novel's
climax. In each, characters have retained no memory of their past
meetings, yet must recover those memories as a means (the only means)
of understanding, confronting, and surviving the unknown. In each,
the characters must reassemble, rediscover their individual and group
identities, and use the strengths inherent in those relationships to ensure
their survival. In each, the truth they rediscover is stranger than anything they could have imagined. And in each, the authors extrapolate
beyond dark fantasy and into science fiction: the monster is in fact an
alien.

At this point, King and Koontz diverge. In the same letter
cited above, Koontz commented that the most important difference be-

tween him and King is King's "tendency toward pessimism and my generally optimistic thematic base. No matter how many ways we may be similar—or different—it is that one difference that, to my mind, will forever make us very dissimilar writers."

And in fact, the natures of the spacefarer in each novel define this fundamental difference. King's is a Lovecraftian horror from unknown worlds, something from the beginning of time that has preyed on human life and human fear, that rises each twenty-seven years to replay its tragedy of human suffering (to this degree, it resembles the protean, omnivorous creature in *Phantoms*). Koontz's aliens, the other hand, are positive. In their final moments, they pass incredible gifts to an unsuspecting humanity, and in the process of discovering the nature of those gifts, the characters in *Strangers* simultaneously define what humanity is and the degree to which they now exceed their own definitions.

Yet in another sense, *IT* and *Strangers* not only diverge but ultimately coincide. In *IT*, for the first time in his major fictions, King allows for an optimistic ending. Evil is destroyed and humanity reaffirmed, sexuality altered from something destructive into a force for regeneration and life. "IT" nearly wins—but at the last, the human impulses defeat it; there is none of the uneasy ambiguity of *Christine*, as Dennis Guilder reads about an odd death in a California drive-in. Certainly there is none of the gruesome horror of the final word of *Pet Sematary*, surely the darkest and most horrifying line King has written.

Instead, *IT* promises peace and fulfillment. Memories fade, but this time the fading has a mythic quality, a power that allies the novel with *Strangers*: characters have changed, as any encounter with the unknown and the extra-human must surely change us.

What we see in *Invasion*, then, is clearly not the attempt of a lesser writer to capitalize on the style and technique of a more successful one. Quite the contrary. In King and Koontz we see two contemporaries, developing at roughly the same time, exploring the possibilities of science fiction and fantasy. Their goals were similar; so were their techniques. To recognize this is not to disparage either King or Koontz, but rather to emphasize the importance of the genre itself as reflecting the concerns—obsessions?—of their world...and ours.

V.

IN THE MIDST OF LIFE

BY RICHARD LAYMON

Hemingway wrote that all stories end in death, and he is no true writer who would keep that from you.

The writer of horror fiction doesn't keep that from you.

Nosirree, Bob.

He rubs your nose in it. His book is a carnival of death, a grisly funhouse.

Leering and chuckling, he takes you by the hand and gives you a guided tour. *Nothing to fear, my friends; it's all in good fun.* And saying that, slides your finger into the wet and eyeless socket of a dead man.

He leads you through the shadows, pointing out the severed head, the disemboweled cadaver, the woman nailed to the wall. He whispers, *Could happen to you*—and titters.

He revels in your fear and disgust as you behold each grisly display.

He is the dark magician of the funhouse, there to amaze and shock.

Dean Koontz is such a magician.

He leads you by the hand down gloomy corridors, shows you the corners where monsters lurk, and takes you into rooms littered with the sloppy remains, whispering, *Watch your step. Some of this may be slippery.*

He shocks you, astounds you, terrifies you with his assortment of grim illusions.

Finally, he cocks an eyebrow and offers to show you the loft. He explains, with some pride, that the loft is the heart of his funhouse.

Oh, boy!

He leads the way up a dark staircase and opens the door.

Sunlight blasts into the corridor. Squinting, you peer into the brightness. A dog dashes forward. But it doesn't foam at the mouth— it seems to be grinning around the copy of *Modern Bride* in its teeth and it wags its tail, eager for fun.

What the hell is going on here?

80

This isn't Cujo, it's Einstein, the golden retriever of *Watchers*, a creature to love, not abhor. In telling about Einstein, who was created by scientists experimenting with recombinant DNA, the character Lem says, "If we can do these amazing things, if we can bring such a wonder into the world, then there's something of profound value in us no matter what the pessimists and doomsayers believe. If we can do this, we have the power and, potentially, the wisdom of God." (2:168).

In the heart of Dean Koontz's house of horrors, we are shown that life holds such treasures as Einstein, miracles of joy and wonder.

Mankind, in the words of Slim MacKenzie, the goblin killer of *Twilight Eyes*, is a "poor, sick, sorry, and much put-upon race." (1:260). But Dean reminds us that, in spite of all that man must suffer, there are moments of glory.

The horror in his books arises out of the evil that threatens to destroy the splendor of life—evil usually created by mankind. Again, Slim MacKenzie:

> If there *was* a God, I could almost understand (as never before) why He would visit pain and suffering upon us. Looking down in disgust at our use of the world and the life He gave us, He might very well say, *All right, you ungrateful wretches, all right! You like to screw up everything? You like to hurt one another? You like it so much you make your own devils and turn them loose on yourselves? All right! So be it!* (1:243)

Man, subverting the gifts of life, creates the monsters that inhabit the dark rooms of the funhouse. In *Shadowfires*, Eric Leben indeed made his own devil and turns it loose—on himself and a host of others. The villain of *Strangers* is a paternal, misguided government running amok over the lives of innocent citizens. Man in pursuit of better weaponry created the murderous goblins of *Twilight Eyes*, the bloodthirsty Outsider of *Watchers*. The horror in each of those four books arises out of man's misuse of his knowledge and/or power.

Without such perversion—if man did not "like to screw up everything" and "like to hurt one another," there would be far less pain and suffering.

In the loft room of the funhouse, Dean Koontz shows us the possibilities. The dog, Einstein, is an example of what man is capable of achieving. Einstein gives us, in the words of Lem, "this incredible sense that mankind is on its way to godhood—and that we *deserve* to get there." (2:169).

The qualities that lift man toward godhood are evident throughout these books. They are stated clearly in a verse from *The Book of Counted Sorrows* at the beginning of Part III of *Strangers*:

Courage, love, friendship
Compassion, and empathy
Lift us above the simple beasts
And define humanity (2:451)

Dean Koontz's books are rich with portrayals of courage, love, friendship, compassion, and empathy. In *Shadowfires*, for example, we find not only the love and courage of the two protagonists, Rachael and Ben, but also the humanity of characters in lesser roles.

There is the police officer Julio Verdad. Every murder is a personal affront to this man, every investigation a crusade:

> Sometimes he said, "Reese, I feel a special commitment to this victim 'cause he was so young, never had a chance to know life, and it isn't fair, it *eats* at me." And sometimes he said, "Reese, this case is personal and if we don't go an extra mile to protect our elderly citizens, then we're a very sick society; this eats at me, Reese." Sometimes the case was special to Julio because the victim was pretty, and it seemed such a tragedy for any beauty to be lost to the world that it just ate at him. But he could be equally eaten because the victim was ugly, therefore already disadvantaged in life, which made the additional curse of death too unfair to be borne.... Julio had such a deep reservoir of compassion and empathy that he was always in danger of drowning in it. (3:114).

Julio Verdad's commitment is to be admired, as is the loyalty of his partner, Reese, who "would have walked away from a million-dollar inheritance sooner than he would have walked away from his partner." (3:115).

Another "minor" character in *Shadowfires* who exhibits the finest qualities of mankind is Ben's war buddy, Whitney Gavis. Gavis is one of humanity's maimed, his face having been brutally disfigured and an arm and leg blown off in war. But his suffering has not diminished his soul. His loyalty to his friend is such that he risks his life for the woman Ben loves. "Benny and me are committed to each other," he tells Rachael, "have been ever since Nam, as good as brothers, better than brothers." (p. 365). Motivated only by his commitment to Ben, this one-armed, one-legged man makes a stand against the beast. Still another hero in *Shadowfires* is Jerry Peake, agent and seeming lackey of his supervisor, the corrupt Anson Sharp. Peake is a naive idealist who reads mystery fiction and dreams of becoming a legend in the department. As he passes through his trial by fire, however, the romance of his job is burned away. As the end approaches, "Peake had given up all hope of becoming a legend.... All he wanted was to get through this night alive to prevent whatever killing he could, and to avoid humiliating himself." (3:394) This is such stuff as humanity is made of.

Jerry Peake is one of our poor, sick, sorry, and much put-upon race. He is no superman, just an ordinary guy. He wants to survive at any cost. And in the end he lifts himself into the realms of heroism because of his desire to "prevent whatever killing he could."

Unlike Whitney Gavis, Jerry Peake is not motivated by love or friendship; those whose lives he wants to save are strangers. He is guided only by his sense of rightness, his empathy, and compassion for fellow human beings.

So he makes his stand. He risks his life for his ideals—and in the process he realizes his dream of becoming a legend. Julio Verdad, Whitney Gavis, and Jerry Peake reside with Einstein and many others in the bright warm loft of the funhouse kept by Dean Koontz for the display of that which is to be cherished in life.

There, too, we find Parker Faine of *Strangers*, an artist whose gusto for life is mammoth, and yet who is willing to risk all for the sake of his friends.

We find Slim MacKenzie of *Twilight Eyes*, a man who has dedicated his life to fighting a one-man battle against the goblins that delight in the pain and death of humans.

We find men and women of courage, who love each other, who love their friends; men and women who care about the fate of strangers; who know right from wrong; who love life and yet are willing to sacrifice themselves for the right. Because that is what makes them human.

Instead of beasts.

Ironically enough, Dean Koontz's most "human" characters, those who portray the very best, those closest to "godhood," are not members of mankind at all.

They are eight creatures from a planet 32,000 light-years from Earth.

Strangers.

These aliens, strangers from outer space, devoted their entire existence, sacrificed their lives, to carry the gifts of knowledge and healing across the vast reaches of the universe—for the sake of strangers.

Ginger Weiss, a surgeon and one of the few to learn the truth about these travelers,

> ...found herself shaking again, as she had shaken
> upon first turning her gaze upon the ancient ship. She
> touched the nearest of the milky-blue containers,
> which seemed to her to be a powerful testimony to

> compassion and empathy beyond human understand-
> ing, the embodiment of a sacrifice that staggered the
> mind and humbled the heart. To have willingly given
> up the comforts of home, to have left their world and
> all their kind to travel such distances on the mere *hope*
> of being able to help a struggling species.... (4:523)

Though the aliens did not survive their voyage, they succeeded
in their mission: they made contact with another race of intelligent beings, mankind, and passed on their knowledge and healing powers.

There would be no more need for medicine and surgery. Human life spans would be extended hundreds of years due to the sacrifice
of these ancient creatures from a distant planet.

"Except for accidents, the specter of death would be banished
to a distant horizon." (4:526)

These eight travelers serve as symbols of mankind's greatest
potential. Like Julio Verdad, Whitney Gavis, Jerry Peake, Parker
Faine, Slim MacKenzie, and so many other characters created by Dean
Koontz, they attempt to banish the horrors of life through love and
courage and sacrifice.

They dwell in the sunlit loft of Dean's funhouse, surrounded
by the many grim faces of death, and they prevail.

Their presence transforms the house of horrors into a house of
hope.

And transforms Dean's books from penny-dreadfuls to art.

Yes, he leads us through the dark chambers and chuckles as we
squirm at the nasty surprises he has created to shock and frighten us.

But it isn't all fun and games.

He wants us to know.

Death is all around us.

In the midst of life, we are in death.

Could happen to you, he whispers.

Will happen to you.

Then he leads us to the loft, shows us Einstein and lovers and
friends, shows us eight travelers from the distant boundaries of space.

Embodiments of those qualities that give life its richness and
glory.

In the midst of death, we are in life.

Dean Koontz, on page 216 of *Watchers*, tells us this:
"Although the constant shadow of certain death looms over every day,
the pleasures and joys of life can be so fine and deeply affecting that the
heart is nearly stilled with astonishment."

VI.

THE MUTATION OF A SCIENCE FICTION WRITER

BY STAN BROOKS

"...they should have narcs who go around checking on creative writers to see if they are getting hooked on their fantasy worlds, because fashioning a science fiction story-future can be like flying on any plastic fantastic chemical..." (1:6)

—Dean Koontz, 1971

"The second thing about my career that displeases me is the fact that I began as a science fiction writer." (2:22)

—Dean Koontz, 1981

At the age of twenty, Dean Koontz won an *Atlantic Monthly* fiction award. The same year he sold his first short story, "Soft Come the Dragons" to *The Magazine of Fantasy & Science Fiction.* Within the next eight years, Koontz would see two dozen short stories and twenty-two novels published—most in the science fiction genre. And with that accomplishment Koontz was justly awarded the title science fiction writer, which he wore around his neck like a set of dog tags.

At first, those dog tags fit rather comfortably. Koontz was a success. He was young. He was making a living—albeit an unspectacular one—from the symbiosis of his imagination and his typewriter. And during the early years, they were dog tags he wore with more than a little pride.

But something happened.

Koontz began to evolve as a writer. He wanted more. Science fiction was limiting his creative talents, limiting his ability to express the wide range of emotions the muse was whispering from within. Also, the genre was scorned by critics as merely disposable fiction, and although his novels were successful as science fiction went, they faded quickly into oblivion. And it wasn't long before Koontz began to long for the respect, the immortality, and the financial rewards of the popular mainstream writer. It was then that he discovered that those dog tags were made of lead, pulling him down in the literary river in which he was trying to advance:

> ...I had already been typecast by publishers, editors, and critics. Editors are usually reluctant to buy a manuscript from an author who is writing outside of the genre in which he is an established name, for they are worried about confusing book buyers. Many people in the publishing industry underestimate the reading public's intelligence and catholicity. Anyway, after being stuck with the *Science Fiction Writer* label, I knew I faced an exhausting, protracted battle to be recognized as simply a writer, period. (2:24)

He decided to completely break from science fiction. To cover his footsteps he bought back the rights to fifteen of the eighteen books he had published in the genre. *Demon Seed* was the last book Koontz published that could be considered purely science fiction, and ironically it was his most successful, and the first to be produced by the motion picture industry.

Through perseverance and considerable talent, Dean Koontz has erased the science fiction writer label. His feet are well-soaked in the mainstream of literature and his name turns up with frequency on the bestseller lists. His writing crosses genres and is equally embraced by suspense, mystery, and horror fiction readers. But was his break from science fiction really that complete? A look through some of those eighteen early novels just might help answer that question. It seems that science fiction writers have always had a fascination with religion. Dean Koontz, far from being an exception, frequently chose themes built around the concept of religion.

> ...I was searching for an understanding of humankind's purpose, our reason for being, our relationship to creation. How do we fit in? Are we the beloved creations of a God? The playthings of a God? Creatures of natural evolution who *invented* a God? Are there morals given in the universe as real—or realer—than the laws of physics? Or do we make our morality as we go? (3)

Being a creator himself, Koontz built future worlds to include future theologies, where often man has become Godlike. Such is the case in *The Flesh in the Furnace*, where a race of spider-men, the Vonopoens, have learned the secret of the creation of life, which they sell to traveling merchants in the form of an easily transportable furnace. Their holy book, *The Book of Wisdom*, is brought to earth along with the teachings of their saints....

> The identity of God changes, as his children unseat him. Each generation, we come under the hand of a fledgling deity who has gained his power through fratricide. This explains why God is clumsy and why his wisdom has never equaled that of his creations: He never had a full lifetime in which to learn.
>
> Saint Zenopau (4:65)

> We can rejoice in our humanity, for there will come a day when God's creatures will have grown more powerful than he. Then we will rise up and dethrone him and his children, and the magic of life-death suspension will be ours. This is not a threat to the divine powers, merely a statement of ecological progression.
>
> Saint Eclesian (4:66)

> God is the mark. We are the con-men. One day we will pull the shuffle on him, and then history will really begin my brothers—and my sisters. Then history will begin with fury!
>
> Saint Eclesian (4:72)

The writings of Saint Zenopau and the Rogue Saint Eclesian lay a groundwork of philosophy for much of Koontz's science fiction. Man versus God. Man competing with God, trying through technology to attain the divine power; the power over life.

There would seem to be two avenues man could take in his quest for divinity: by conquering death, or unlocking the secret of creation. Both are explored by Koontz, but it is the second in which he seemed to have held the greatest fascination—a fascination that he would carry with him over the borders of horror and mainstream writing. In his 1970 novel *Dark of the Woods*, Koontz describes a paradise world once ruled by peaceful winged-people, the Demosians. The Demosians developed an artificial womb, which enabled them to regenerate still-living cells from the recently deceased into new bodies.

They had discovered the divine power—artificial creation of life, and, at the same time, the conquest of death. This power, which brings mortal beings to a Godlike level, is found regularly in Koontz's science fiction. And a few times, Koontz has allowed man to surpass God.

In his novel *A Darkness in My Soul*, expanded from his short story of the same name, man has done just that. It is the story of Simeon Kelly, a product of the artifical wombs who has the ability to

travel into the minds of others. The world is on the verge of a holo-
caustal war, and the means of preventing annihilation may lie within the
vast subsconscious mind of Child, another product of the artifical
wombs. But Child remains mute, withdrawn into a world he has created within the vast intellect of his mind. The government contracts
Simeon to travel into Child's mind and retrieve any information that
may save the world. There, Simeon finds a universe created by Child,
a universe in which Child is master: God. He eventually learns that
Child has reached the mind of God himself, along with a darker revelation—*God is insane*. For centuries man has wondered why a sane God
would allow cataclysm after cataclysm devastate his creation. And man
answered that it was his divine test, a test of courage to see how man
could cope, strengthen. But the fact was that God had merely gone insane, an insanity brought upon him by extreme loneliness. Simeon, in
essence, kills both Child and God by bleeding energy away and meshing it with his own psychic power. By killing God, Simeon becomes
God:

> I felt no remorse.
> Does one feel remorse when one shoots down a
> maniac who is wielding a gun in a crowded depart-
> ment store?
> Man as God. I retained the mortal form and the
> mortal outlook, with the emotions and prejudices of
> men. I did not think that would be a weakness, but
> that it might actually make me a more benevolent and
> stable deity than the previous owner of my power had
> been. Man as God... (5:109)

Simeon learns from God's mistake, and transmits half of his
newfound powers to a female partner. Each with half the power of the
previous God, they set off to rule the universe. For ten thousand years
they roam the corners of existence learning of the world they inherited.
Finally, they become bored and decide to let Earth know of their existence.

> And though we had ended the rivalries of reli-
> gions, we went down to Earth to revive them. We
> brought forth temples and synagogues, churches and
> altars, and garish robes and bejeweled priests. We
> created hierarchies of worthless prelates and we spoke
> our words to the masses through the mouths of men of
> less value than most other men. (6:123)

As Simeon and his partner become bored again, they revive hatred and warfare, and soon the world is no different than it had been in previous centuries under previous rule. Man as God....

But if man can ultimately surpass the powers of God with his own creations, can't those creations ultimately surpass the powers of man? According to Dean Koontz, the answer is decidely yes. In his earlier mentioned work, *The Flesh in the Furnace,* the puppets, miniature creations of human life, become dissatisfied with their existence. They are tired of "performing" for their "God," the puppetmaster. They have the puppetmaster killed, and in time conquer the Earth. Eventually, they conquer other worlds as well. The Vonopoens use the furnace to create a loyal warrior race of creatures which then destroy the puppets. And so the cycle continues.

And what would the Vonopoen Rogue Saint Eclesian say about this....

> We Vonopoens have long prided ourselves on what we think of as our highest artform, our realistic miniature puppets. We make them in our own images and in the images of animals and other races, and we have them perform for us. Perhaps if we spent less time playing Gods in this respect and examined the universe more closely, we would discover that we are all only puppets ourselves, on a much greater scale. We have our scripts. There are repetitious cycles. And somewhere, I think, there are voices that laugh at us. Even at me.
>
> Saint Eclesian (4:132)

In Koontz's other science fiction novels, God turns up as a major character.

In *Anti-Man,* God turns out to be an alien intelligence so vast that only a part of him can inhabit our universe at one time. He visits the Earth in the form of an android, with the intention of passing on some of his powers mankind.

In Koontz's comic science fiction supernatural detective novel, *The Haunted Earth,* God turns out to be a rather pathetic character who is a regular at nightclubs, guests on talk shows (where he is humiliated), and admits to orgies in heaven.

As he and his writing matured, Koontz dropped the "what is God" struggle from his novels, but a strong sense of the spiritual has continued into his horror fiction.

> Well, after all these years of mulling over the subject, I have formed the belief that humankind evolved—as did the universe—under the guidance of

some greater consciousness and that we have a purpose and a destiny that we do not yet understand but
that we must gradually discover and pursue. I suspect
that our destiny might be to become gods ourselves, a
theme that surely is obvious in some recent books like
Strangers and *Watchers*. (3)

Man cannot fashion life in his image from clay and divine
breath. He doesn't have to, he's got recombinant DNA—the genetic
blueprint of life etched indelibly within his own cells. And it is the
blueprint for more than one of Koontz's later works, especially his
Leigh Nichols suspense novels.

In *The Eyes of Darkness*, recombinant DNA research is carried
out secretly by the military in an effort to create biological weapons. In
The House of Thunder, the government is secretly funding the milestone
project to create biological and other weapons. In *Shadowfires*, a scientist is able to defeat death through the rejuvenation of his own cells
by altering his DNA—and, oh yes, the government has agents after
him. In *Watchers*, DNA research has produced the most advanced biological weapon yet, a monstrous killing machine brought to us cour-
tesy of—the government. Now, it's obvious that these four novels have
something in common, and what they have most in common is not the
obvious, for they are each very different tales.

Horror.

To Dean Koontz, horror is achieved by placing the ultimate
weapon in the hands of the ultimate madmen. Not to say that all government men are made, but the government, particularly the military
and intelligence agencies, provides a petry dish in which madness can
thrive, and madmen can attain high seats of authority. They sometimes
operate on group-think, where rationality can take a back seat to "the
good of the mission."

Koontz understands this well. His protagonists are just as
likely to do battle with a government agent as with a lizard-skinned
monster. And that agent may be just as horrifying.

In the Leigh Nichols novel, *The Eyes of Darkness*, the government is trying to discover why a thirteen-year-old boy, accidentally
infected with a deadly Soviet-engineered virus—Gorki 400—has survived. To enable them to study the boy—by re-infecting him with the
virus—the government has its secret security agency, Network, fake his
death in a staged accident. His mother and her lover discover that there
has been a cover-up and set out to find him. The Network, lead by its
ruthless leader, George Alexander, intends to stop the pair by killing
them.

Alexander justifies the murder of innocent people, who just
happen to get in the way of national security, as his patriotic duty. But
more than that, it gives him a spiritual power.

For as long as he could remember, he had been fascinated with death, with the mechanics and the meaning of it, and he had longed to know what it was like on the other side—without, of course, wanting to commit himself to a one-way journey there. He didn't want to die; he only wanted to know. Each time that he personally killed someone, he felt as though he were establishing another link to the world beyond this one; and he hoped, once he made enough of those linkages, that he would be rewarded with a vision from the other side. One day, maybe he would be standing in a graveyard, before the tombstone of one of his victims, and the person he killed would reach out to him from beyond and let him see, in some vivid clairvoyant fashion, exactly what death was like. And then he would know. (6:306)

Alexander has the dark power to bring death, which means, in a way, that he has the power over life. In the warped interiors of his mind, this power makes him Godlike. It is a delusion Koontz has placed in the minds of a few of Alexander's literary colleagues.

In *Watchers*, Vince Nasco is an American assassin working for the Soviet government. He is probably the most ruthless, cold-blooded character to slash his way through a Koontz novel. He's dangerous because he kills not for patriotic pride, not for money, but for immortality. He believes that a small portion of the life force of his victims is absorbed within him after each assasination. His dream is to murder a pregnant woman, so that he may absorb the virgin energy of an unborn life.

Such assassins play a less prominent role in Koontz's science fiction, but they made occasional appearances. And, as in his later fiction, some were government agents. In his short story, "The Psychedelic Children," the futuristic American government—The Constitutional Tolerant Party—employs both android and human agents to eliminate the Hallucino-Children. These are the descendants of people who regularly used LSD in the 1960s and '70s, and who have gained, through mutation, psychic powers deemed dangerous by the government.

In his 1969 novel, *The Fall of the Dream Machine*, Koontz brings us a world almost ruled by the electronic media. There is no television. There is SHOW, experienced by seven hundred million subscribers daily. SHOW is a complete sensory experience. Subscribers do not simply watch actors playing roles; they become the actors. They see what the actors see, think the same thoughts, share the same tactile sensations. It has made media addicts of the world, and there is but one pusher, Alexander Cockley, the director of SHOW. He is an evil man who seeks to rule the world; a deadly man who enjoys ordering others to their deaths. And long before Freddy Krueger, of *The Nightmare on Elm Street*, Alexander Cockley had razor-sharp, retractable steel blades in his fingers, which he uses with deadly accuracy to persuade others to his way of thinking.

The horrors in these novels do not ascend from the depths of slimy swamps; they need not turn into bats or wolves, or boogey-eyed monsters. They are just men, controlled by other men, and they are scary as hell.

In comparing these evil men, often turned to evil deed from the group-think mentality, there is one major difference between those appearing in Koontz's science fiction and his later novels. In his horror and suspense books, these men are generally renegades. They may work for the government, but they are involved in agencies so classified and subclassified that they no longer represent attitudes of the government at all—assuming of course that the government is ruled by sane men.

Therefore, once these men are beaten and exposed, the hope remains that others will not be able to abuse the power given them. At the end of the novel, we return to the free people we are meant to be, living in a free society. Throughout these books, there is always hope.

Not so in Koontz's science fiction.

Generally, these books take place far enough into the future that the government has been unrecognizably restructured—or for that matter, the government might well be an alien one. Often, this governmental restructuring is secondary to some cataclysmic event, which forces society to give up the freedoms we take for granted. Evil men in these books are not renegades: they represent a world different from our own. They have different values, an alien code of ethics. The world has changed. And even if the protagonists manage to escape into the mountains and be free of the sadistic military leader of the "Earth Alliance," "World Federational Government," or whichever—the fact is that nothing has really changed in the end. The madness has not been beaten, merely temporarily outsmarted. The oppression continues. Many times, early in such futuristic novels, hope is lost.

Hope. Hopelessness.
Optimism. Pessimism.

These are perspectives that, more often than not, differ science fiction from horror and mainstream fiction. And they are perspectives that differ the Koontz of 1970 from the Koontz of today.

> My books are about the great value of the individual (if each of us has within him the destiny to be God, how could he be anything but valuable?), about the love relationships between mates and friends and relatives. With this philosophy, I am of course a

thorough-going optimist, a believer in people and in the future, and my optimism makes my fiction considerably different from that of nearly anyone else I can think of in the dark-suspense, dark-fantasy genres, where misanthropy of one degree or another colors the work of virtually every writer. (3)

Certainly, one reason for the change from pessimism to optimism is the fact that his science fiction novels were written during a time of social upheaval. The war in Vietnam was seemingly endless. Political assassinations were a commonly reported event on the evening news. The climate was right for social rebellion. And the natural way for a young writer to join that rebellion was through the power of the pen. The oppressed people may have been alien and winged instead of black, assassinations may have been carried out by androids instead of men, but the themes were often merely a reflection of that decade of social turbulence.

Still...

It seems that science fiction lends itself well to a feeling of pessimism. Even if it's not the intent of the writer to project a gloomy atmosphere, it is often unavoidable. People are more comfortable in familiar surroundings. They relate better to characters that they are familiar with, can empathize with. It's just not easy for us to feel strongly about what becomes of an android or mutant; even if they prevail, they're still going to be a damned android or mutant. Koontz's work became more optimistic from the moment he left the science fiction genre. Although his earliest diversions were pure horror, some under his Owen West moniker, in which very horrible things happen to some nice people, a feeling of hope even persisted throughout these novels.

In *The Funhouse*, we know that death lurks in the traveling carnival. We know that Amy Harper is the target of the horror that haunts the funhouse, that this horror has been patiently waiting for her since before her birth, waiting to avenge a wrong her mother had committed twenty-five years before. And we know—we hope—that Amy will eventually enter that funhouse and confront the horror. But we also know that if she can prevail, if she can survive, she will have a bright future. Optimism. Hope. We care about Amy Harper. We've all known someone like her.

In one of Koontz's most terrifying books, *Darkfall*, the horror comes from the very depths of Hell. In this horror novel, Koontz has created a tale as grim as any you are likely to read. The atmosphere is bleak throughout, where we enter a world of organized crime, drug dealing, and voodoo priests. An evil practioner of Vodun uses his black arts to conjure up a few creatures from Hell to act as invincible hit men, to aid him in taking over the drug trade from a Mafia family in

New York. But he opens the gates of Hell too wide, and what results is a murderous rampage. A rampage carried out by demons. And it is up to two city cops to stop it.

Sound hopeless enough? Not really.

It is hope that holds us to the novel. Hope that good will prevail, no matter how powerful the evil. Koontz is a master at raising those hopes and then unexpectedly dropping them into the depths from which his demons have risen.

> In St. Patrick's Cathedral, Rebecca took two steps toward the piles of now-ordinary earth that had, only a moment ago, been living creatures, but she stopped short when the scattered dirt trembled with a current of impossible perverse life. The stuff wasn't dead after all. The grains and clots and clumps of soils seemed to draw moisture from the air; the stuff became damp; the separate pieces in each loose pile began to quiver and strain and draw laboriously toward the others. This evilly enchanted earth was apparently trying to regain its previous forms, struggling to reconstitute the goblins. One small lump, lying apart from all the others, began to shape itself into a tiny, wickedly clawed foot.
> "Die, damnit," Rebecca said. "Die!" (7:367)

Yet he holds us by that thread, that strong filament of optimism, that if only the cops can discover the secret, if only the Voodoo priest can be outsmarted, the world will return to normal and the characters live happily ever after.

It is hope which keeps us imprisoned in the tale, but it is the tale itself which must first capture us. And as jailer, Koontz seems to have imprisoned a wider audience since leaving the science fiction genre. And it was his horror fiction which brought critical acclaim, and it was this genre which launched him into the mainstream of literature.

The horror genre gave Koontz the freedom he needed to exercise literary muscles left to atrophy in his science fiction.

In science fiction, it is often the *science* that takes up the writer's energy. In a sea of robotix and computer chips, alien warriors and post-holocaustal disease, characterization can be left to drift aimlessly. Plots may not be strong enough to hold up under the weight of futuristic technology, which may serve to stretch but also tenuate the imagination.

In horror fiction, on the other hand, we know, or are intimately involved in, the world in which the story is taking place. We therefore care about this world. We can relate more closely to the characters and the emotions they express, and more importantly, so does the author.

By shunting his creative energy from amazing the reader with a futuristic world of technology, Koontz has sharply honed his characterization skills. Most of his characters are ordinary people with ordinary careers catapulted into extraordinary situations. We can laugh with them, cry with them, shiver in fear with them, and even, sometimes, very much hate them, because we *know* them. And that's something that's difficult to say about an alien lizard man from Pluto, no matter how much work the author has put into the character.

When a novel's characters are universally appealing, when the plot is strong and the action jam-packed, that novel will find a wide audience. And when there's a wide audience, the critics will notice. And while Koontz has not won all the critics over, he has certainly won their attention.

But has Koontz really left science fiction entirely?

Yes, ideas from my science fiction have crept into my latter work, but not consciously. I never set out to take elements used in early SF novels and rework them in a mainstream context. I've too many new ideas to bother looking toward the past for inspiration. (3)

It would seem that those eighteen early science fiction novels may have dropped a few seeds into Koontz's fertile imagination. As discussed earlier, the idea of life created outside the womb appeared repeatedly in his science fiction and has appeared in some of his horror-suspense novels as well. Subliminal suggestion, the theme of *Night Chills*, popped up in his science fiction: it was prominent in *Demon Seed* and *The Fall of the Dream Machine*. *The Vision*, *The Face of Fear*, and *The Mask* all have characters who possess psychic powers, but so did the science fiction novels, *A Darkness in My Soul* and *Time Thieves*.

Strangers has appeared on all the bestseller lists. It is an epic tale of cross-genre appeal. But science fiction—although not until late in the novel—plays a significant role in the plot's twist. Science fiction finds a place in the plots of *Watchers* and *Shadowfires*. But none of these novels could be considered in the science fiction genre. They cover a broad literary spectrum. The strength of the story lies within the characterization and plot, and not with the technology. They are action novels, horror novels, suspense novels, romance novels, *mainstream novels*. Dean Koontz does not write in a vacuum, and the fact is that you don't write eighteen science fiction novels and not like the genre, so it seems that he's not likely to abandon it completely. And while he may no longer be flying on his plastic, fantastic chemical, like any ex-addict, he had to go through a period of withdrawal and he's bound to have an occasional flashback or two. But Koontz has accomplished what he set out to—he's not a science fiction writer, not even a horror writer, but simply a *successful* writer.

VII.

MAINSTREAM HORROR IN *WHISPERS* AND *PHANTOMS*

BY D. W. TAYLOR

"Whether we realize it or not," Dean Koontz once told an interviewer, "we write about what we are, where we've been, and what we're afraid of" (5:23). It should come as no surprise, then, to find *Whispers* and *Phantoms* filled with characters who have become in their adult lives the walking wounded of child abuse. In that same interview, Koontz describes his own life with a violent, alcoholic father who cast a giant shadow of fear over his entire childhood, a darkness that Koontz admits, "...has affected my work immensely" (5:23).

Koontz draws deeply upon this personal background for the thematic structures of both these novels, where the protagonists and sometimes even the villains are haunted by the abuse and lovelessness they experienced as children. Both works chart the main characters' attempts to overcome these early traumas that cripple them now as adults. Indeed, the plots of both books, including their horrific elements, do not merely furnish action and suspense; they also serve as vehicles for the characters' often painful discovery of truth about themselves and their pasts. This blend of mainstream fiction's emphasis on character, together with horror fiction's emphasis on suspense, gives *Whispers* and *Phantoms* something unique: a one-two emotional punch that enables the novels to be both deeply moving and thrilling at the same time, in a prose style that ranges from the delicately rendered moment of epiphany to the all-out, in-your-face terror alert.

The trappings of the horror novel, especially the investigation of evil and final confrontation with it, are closely woven into the fabric of what are essentially mainstream novels of character. Each step the characters take toward uncovering the truth about the evil which threatens them is paralleled on an emotional plane, where they are simultaneously coming closer and closer to discovering the truth about themselves. This journey to the heart of darkness, a convention of the horror novel, becomes for Koontz's characters a journey into themselves. And at the climax of the novels, where according to horror convention the source of evil must be uncovered and thwarted, Koontz melds together these two plot lines of the emotional and the horrific into intensely powerful moments of resolution. Not only is the evil which threatens them defeated, but the characters achieve another kind of victory in the process—triumph over the personal demons that once ruled their lives.

1. THE WHISPERING UNDEAD

The demons are many in the lives of those troubled characters who inhabit the world of *Whispers*. Although physically dead, these evil spirits remain very much alive in memory, and wreak very real havoc in the characters' lives. Koontz has taken a potentially stale device of the horror genre—the undead—and kept it alive by borrowing from mainstream realism. These are not supernatural evil spirits, but worse: ones that can and do exist for everyone in the ultimate landscape of horror, the mind.

When Hilary's agent tells her, "Your parents are gone. Dead. They can't touch you.... They can't hurt you ever again" (4:20-21), he is forgetting that our childhoods can haunt us as adults, preventing us from realizing our potentials and from finding happiness and intimacy. The dead do live on in the everyday lives of these characters, and unless the living can loosen the hold that the undead still have on them, people like Hilary are doomed to a circumscribed life, confined forever within a haunted house of memory.

Appropriately, Koontz allows a mortician to sum up the role that the undead play in our lives:

> "What I've come to learn, is that you've got to
> treat the dead with every bit as much concern as you
> do the living. You can't just put them out of mind,
> bury them and forget about them. All the things they
> did to us are still in our minds, still shaping and
> changing us. So in a way, the dead never really die at
> all" (309-10).

Supposedly, Bruno Frye is insane because he believes his mother has come back from the dead in someone else's body and now plots to kill him. But in a profound and tragic way, Bruno is quite correct: his mother is very much alive and at work in his life, her memory torturing him every day, driving him to brutal acts of rape and murder. Bruno, like all of the novel's significant characters, is possessed by the "undead."

At times Koontz tries to blur the distinction between the living and the dead. This is certainly true with the Frye brothers. Throughout most of the novel Koontz makes it difficult for Hilary and the reader to know how many Brunos are alive and how many she has

killed, if any. But the blurring is done on more subtle levels as well.
For example, after his first attack Bruno Frye becomes for Hilary her
dead father returned to life: "As before, in a curious dreamlike flux,
the memory of Frye became a memory of her father, so that for an instant she had the crazy notion that it had been Earl Thomas, raised from
the dead, who had tried to kill her tonight" (109). Here, as throughout
the novel, the dead never really die, and until they do, until their spirits
are finally exorcised, the living can never really live.

The novel's main characters, like zombies sleepwalking a
blasted landscape of memory, are in effect controlled from the grave by
specters of their pasts, as if trapped in a strange twilight world of the
half-dead and half-alive. Especially Hilary Thomas. On the surface,
she is a Hollywood screenwriter whose chocolate-brown Mercedes,
fashionable Bel Air address, and designer wardrobe testify to her
success. But it's all window-dressing. Beneath the surface glitter lies
an inescapable darkness, a legacy of child abuse that has left the beautiful Hilary a woman without a sense of self-worth, incapable of happiness and with a hermetic seal over her heart. Her parents, both self-
pitying, bitter alcoholics whose lives ended in a mad bloodbath of uxo-
ricide and suicide, have instilled in her "a quiet but ever-present and
unshakable paranoia that stained everything good, everything that
should be right and bright and joyful" (20-21). So, on the sunlit California coast Hilary has built a beautiful but hollow temple of loneliness
and locked herself in it, alone with the ghosts of her past, a workaholic
waiting for the worst to happen because, in her life, it always has.

And does. Bruno Frye's savage attack and attempted rape
forces back the iron lid that she has pulled over her past. In an instant
he shatters her fragile peace and rips open all the old wounds that a
childhood of neglect and violence inflicted upon her. At first, for both
Hilary and the reader, Bruno Frye is a hideous maniac who elicits our
revulsion and deserves only our contempt. Even his name adds to his
"brutal" image and our loathing of him. However, Koontz is merely
cleverly manipulating another convention of the horror genre, and
preparing to give his villain a depth and sympathy usually found only in
mainstream fiction. The reader is about to discover along with Hilary
that the distinction between victim and victimizer is a fine one indeed.

Koontz lays the groundwork for this carefully and elaborately.
Just as Hilary is sharply aware of "a spectral darkness at the edges of
things" (2), Bruno Frye also has "hideous memories [at] the edge of his
awareness" (104). At the beginning of the novel we are told that Hilary's parents had "jammed her into a tiny box of fear, slammed the
heavy lid and locked it" (20-21); and so for Hilary the world became "a
dangerous place, a shadowy cellar with nightmare creatures" (43).
Likewise, we learn at the end of the novel that Bruno's box of fear, the
opposite bookend of Hilary's, is just such a dark cellar filled with
creatures—swarming roaches. As with Hilary, a parent pushes Bruno

into it, "slams [the door]...locks it" (429). In between the two book-ends, the secrets to both Hilary's and Bruno's past are stacked gradually, in alternation, scene after pathetic scene, revelation after shocking revelation, until finally we understand: Bruno's name signifies not just that he brutalizes others, but also that he, a child of incest, was himself brutalized—horribly and unspeakably. After hearing a tape recording on which a hypnotized and agonizing Bruno reveals his mother's torture of him, we and Hilary realize that "...maybe Frye's a victim, too" (432). The identification between victim and victimizer is completed as Hilary is forced to relive Frye's own horror when she becomes trapped in that same root cellar of the soul, and must fight off the roaches that begin to cover her—just as they once did Frye.

By the end of the novel Koontz has made it possible and even necessary for the reader to transfer the sympathy felt for Hilary, the heroine, to Bruno Frye, the villain, whose death becomes a poignant, unsettling mixture of revenge and relief—for Hilary, the reader, and Bruno. Bruno Frye is not merely a horror novel's stock villain. In the tightly woven fabric of mainstream fiction, he is a victim too, just as the mother who abused him was herself a victim of father-daughter incest. Just as all who carry with them these legacies of the undead are victims.

The legacy that Tony Clemenza must bear, while not as unsavory or perverted, is nonetheless just as powerfully inhibiting. Tony's impoverished childhood and penurious father have bestowed upon Tony an obsession with financial security, making it impossible for him to realize his dream of becoming an artist: "Tony had been so totally indoctrinated, so completely infused with his father's fears and principles" (62-63) that he has become a workaholic of the worst sort: he has sold his soul to the police department and his savings passbook. One can't help but recall that Koontz himself once said: "Having been dirt-poor as a child, I have a deathly fear of poverty," a fear that keeps this best-selling author and self-confessed workaholic even now "edgy about the future" (5:23).

To overcome his anxiety about money, to free himself from the ghost of his father, Tony must find what every character in this novel lacks: a nourishing relationship where two people come together in the bonds of intimacy, trust, and affection to form a whole greater than its parts. It is only in such a relationship that Tony and the others can hope to discover their true selves and potentials that lie buried beneath the crust of the past. Tony forges such a relationship with Hilary: "With you, because of you, for the very first time, I'm willing to take a few tentative steps away from the security of being on the public payroll" (286). He can now seriously consider being an artist without remembering the voice of the undead: "And now I don't always hear Papa's lecture about money and responsibility and the cruelty of fate, like I used to" (286). For Hilary, her relationship with Tony means learning to trust someone again, lowering her protective shield of self-reliance and intense privacy that she erected as a child against her violent and unloving parents. Only the intimacy of lovemaking can penetrate her shield: "This was an important ritual, a profound ceremony that was cleansing her of long-nurtured fears. She was entrusting herself to another human being in a way she would have thought impossible only a week ago" (260).

Koontz uses their relationship to explore the true nature of sexual intimacy, and, in the process, to criticize current promiscuous attitudes. For Tony and Hilary, lovemaking is much more than a vigorous and mutually satisfying workout; it has the potential to be a spiritual as well as a physical joining: "She knew Tony felt it, too, this unique and astonishingly deep bonding. They were physically, emotionally, intellectually, and psychically joined, molded into a single being that was far superior to the sum of its halves" (405). Tony and Hilary become the only survivors in the novel because they are the only two who establish a nourishing, intimate relationship based upon honesty, trust, and mutual respect. Only this kind of relationship can allow them to overcome their crippling pasts and to walk fully upright as humans again. Only this kind of relationship satisfies a universal need: "A hunger for love and comradeship [that] is as natural to our species as the requirement for food and water" (166).

In mainstream fashion, Koontz weaves virtually every character and incident into this thematic structure—the need for intimacy in order to be fully human. The best example is the Frye brothers, whose relationship serves as a photographic reverse image of Hilary and Tony's. Just as the novel is the story of two people, Hilary and Tony, finding each other and coming together as one, it's also the story of two people who were once one, the Frye brothers, being split apart and dying because of it. When Tony says to Hilary, "It's like we were each only half a person—and now we've found our missing halves. We've been knocking around all our lives, groping in the dark, trying to find each other" (287), he has unwittingly discovered the secret of Bruno Frye: he is not one, but two men melded together into a single identity as they groped together in the hellish darkness of the root cellar.

Throughout the novel, Koontz constructs parallel love scenes between these two couples, scenes that when placed beside each other offer a striking contrast of the beautiful with the beautifully grotesque. When Tony makes love to Hilary, "He felt strangely as if he were melting into her, as if they were becoming one creature, not physically or sexually so much as spiritually" (253). The Frye twins are also melted toqether, but for a much different reason: "Under tremendous pressure from their mother, they...melted together psychologically, melted into one. Two individuals with one personality, one self-awareness, one self-image" (470). And when Tony and Hilary make love for the first time, at the peak of a rapturous, soul-fulfilling experience, they stare deeply at one another: "Their eyes locked, and after a moment it seemed that he was no longer merely staring at her, but into her, through her eyes, into the essence of Hilary Thomas, into her soul" (253-54). Contrasted with that is the last time that Bruno sleeps with his brother, now dead. He stares into the other's lifeless eyes, is at first repulsed, but then: "He tried not to look at them but *into* them, deep down beyond the surface ruin, way down in, where (many times in the past) he had made the blazing, thrilling connection with the other half of his soul" (462). Face-to-face, soul-to-soul, the partners of each couple search desperately for the same connection that will keep them alive and make them whole, but one couple is a perverted image of the other.

So elaborate is Koontz's thematic structure, constructed with such care, that it includes even minor characters like Frank Howard, Tony's partner. At first Frank seems the typical Koontz villain—a woman hater who badgers Hilary relentlessly during his interrogation, committing verbal rape of a victim already on the edge of emotional collapse. But Frank's hostility merely masks his own pain, his own inability to establish an intimate and nuturing relationship with a woman, a failing that has turned him into a belligerent misogynist. But Koontz uses Frank to show how warmth and love can rescue even the most bitter of souls. Unable to cope with the death of his first wife, desperate to replace her, Frank allows himself to be fleeced by a gold-digger who tears out his wounded heart and serves it to him for supper one night. Because of that betrayal, Frank's contempt of women and his isolation from normal human feelings grow steadily, endangering himself and others, until Tony reaches out to establish a bond of intimacy that pulls Frank back into the human race and enables him to face his pain.

Frank had even started dating again before he is murdered by Bobby Valdez, another woman-hating rapist, and another example of a minor character woven into the novel's thematic structure. Joshua Rhinehart, a lawyer who aids in unraveling the mystery of the Frye family, is also a minor character who not only contributes to the plot, but to the work's emotional resonance as well. Before his wife's death, Joshua rarely remembers dreaming and never had nightmares. But now he is plagued by dreams in which he searches hopelessly for something terribly important but indescribable: "He didn't need a psychiatrist to tell him that those dreams were about Cora. He still had not adjusted to life without her. Perhaps he never would" (216-17). Joshua's nightmare, Koontz seems to suggest, is our ultimate one: being alone.

Joshua's pain is also a part of another motif which helps to color this novel of dark suspense with a thematic and emotional depth usually associated only with the literary mainstream. Koontz makes it plain that intimacy, openness, genuine caring—the very feelings which make us human and give us joy—can bring great pain as well. Love, in real life as well as in realistic novels, is a double-edged sword. Hilary intuits this fact and has always avoided making friends and finding lovers partly because, "She was afraid of the pain that only friends and lovers could inflict with their rejections and betrayals" (195). And once she does open up to Tony, she begins having dreams of two sorts: of happiness with Tony ("golden and fuzzy around the edges"), but also of the anguish of the Chicago apartment where she was abused (216). So, falling in love means opening up to the whole range of human emotions, letting the good and the bad flow together, and comforting ourselves with the knowledge that it's the flow which keeps us alive. Koontz's characters learn the very real lesson that love is not pablum; the risks can be as great as the rewards. Indeed, after Frank's death, Tony is devasted. Hilary sees the "haunted look in his face and the bleak expression in his eyes" (246). But she is there to comfort him, and the cycle of intimacy continues. It is only after Frank's death that Hilary and Tony can make love for the first time. Out of great pain has come an even greater joy. And so it goes.

Perhaps this is the ultimate meaning of the many whispers which sigh and murmur throughout the novel, rising and falling like *leitmotifs* in a Wagner opera. These whispers, like love itself, like humans themselves, have a dual nature. This most intimate of sounds is used for telling secrets, but these secrets can be good or they can be dark and deadly, telling us of the worst things, the most dreadful things. In this novel there are certainly both kinds—whispers of love and of terror—but they are always whispers of truth that we simultaneously desire yet dread to hear.

For as long as Bruno Frye could remember, he wanted to find out what was whispering in his nightmares, to know the truth of what they were trying to tell him. Yet, "Now that he was on the edge of knowing, he found the knowledge more horrifying and devastating than the mystery had been" (363). Bruno never does acknowledge that the whispers are the sound of the swarming roaches, and perhaps Koontz implies here that the difference between the psychopathic Bruno Frye and others is that to be sane we must be able to face the truth that comes in whispers. For some, like Bruno, there is no hope; the truth is so awful that it could never be faced without obliteration of the self. For others, like Hilary and Tony, the support of an intimate as well as individual courage is needed in order to face the truth.

Whispers also tell the truth about other people and our world. As Tony leaves the apartment of Lana Haverby, a pathetic, burnt-out groupie of the '60s who has never moved beyond adolescence, he glances back to her and listens to "those faint whispering voices that were trying to explain the meaning of her life" (143). And when Frank Howard finally opens up to Tony to share the hurt and betrayal that have nearly turned him into a monster, "His voice was soft, almost a whisper..." (170). These whispers are also insidious: "Fear of the impending catastrophe was an ever-present whisper that propagandized the subconscious mind, a very influential whisper that molded people's attitudes and characters more than they would ever know" (293).

But at the end of this novel about the struggle to hear these faint murmurs of truth about ourselves and our pasts, it is the whisper of happiness and hope that is finally heard. As Tony and Hilary walk away from the root cellar, the ultimate symbol of the dark secrets which lie hidden in our pasts, as they walk away from the dead body of Frye, whose madness and pain paradoxically brought them together, Tony tells Hilary that, "For the first time in our lives, we both know who we are, what we want, and where we're going. We've overcome the past." Having done so, having bravely sought out and understood those whispers, they can now walk together through the cleansing, healing autumn rain as it "hammered softly on them and whispered in the grass" (502).

2. THE COSMIC FAMILY OF *PHANTOMS*

Jenny Paige's nightmare officially begins as she clutches a telephone in a barricaded room filled with the hideous, bloated corpses of her friends. She senses the silent phantoms all around her and feels suddenly as if "an enormously heavy iron cover were being slid off a dark pit in her subconscious. In that pit, within ancient chambers of the mind, there lay a host of primitive sensations and perceptions" (2:56).

Thus, at the beginning of this story, Jenny Paige, just as Hilary Thomas did, must face the threat of annihilation, a threat which reduces life to its most primitive elements. Terror is again being used, as it was in *Whispers*, to strip away the thin veneer of civilization which barely separates the young, attractive heroine from a deeper and uglier part of herself. "Now," Koontz seems to be saying as he rubs his hands together in sadistic glee, "let's see what these humans are made of. Let's see how they survive the horrors that I'm about to inflict upon them." In *Whispers*, survival comes through the strength found in the intimate, nurturing relationships between a man and a woman. In *Phantoms*, survival comes through the strong bonding that takes place among members of a nuclear family, which is the human pressure point that Koontz probes with his very sharp instrument.

In an important way *Phantoms* is a sequel to *Whispers*. Both are essentially realistic novels where terror and suspense are devices used to set in motion the characters' search for truth about themselves and their world. With *Phantoms*, Koontz has again written a novel that is more about self-discovery and growth than about horror. He again merely borrows the trappings of the horror/suspense genre, this time with a slight supernatural coloring, as background for a study of individuals. Playing a featured role in this novel, however, are the family unit and its crucial function in the lives of individuals. At its thematic core, *Phantoms* is the story of disintegrated families and of the scattered individual survivors seeking to reknit their lives within the fabric of a new and viable family.

All of the protagonists are woven into this structure. Lisa Paige, for instance, is a teenager who suddenly finds herself without a family. She never knew her father, who died when she was two, and has recently been traumatized by discovering her mother's lifeless body in the kitchen of their home. Anguished and reeling from the *loss* of the only family she has ever really known, Lisa must now turn to her alienated sister, Jenny, a woman who is virtually a stranger. When this sister brings Lisa to the extended family of Snowfield, the first thing Lisa encounters in the kitchen of her new home is yet another woman's dead body. Her nightmare continues. And just as Koontz himself once had to, Lisa becomes a child who must find a strength beyond her years to combat the violence and horror that have invaded her family and threaten to overwhelm her.

Jenny Paige, like Hilary Thomas in *Whispers*, is also a woman on the run from family violence, playing a child's game of hide-and-seek with her past. But unlike the lonely and vulnerable Hilary, Jenny has found a substitute family in the close-knit community of Snowfield. Jenny flourishes in her role as the matriarchal family physician, feeling a sense of belonging for the first time in a long time. But Jenny's tender maternal care of her new family is, in large measure, merely her way of dealing with the guilt that plagues her.

Jenny has avoided her real home for many years because she *sees* in her mother's eyes the accusation: *"You killed your father, Jenny; you broke his heart, and that killed him"* (68). At eighteen, Jenny defied her parents by "living in sin" with and eventually marrying Campbell Hudson, an older man who, like all of the villains in *Phantoms* and *Whispers*, is a woman-hater and abuser. When "Cam" savagely pummels Jenny into a miscarriage, committing what is the ultimate sin in this novel by killing a child and rending the fabric of a family irreparably, Jenny's life becomes an attempt to expiate the guilt she feels over the *loss* of her own child and her father's death. In her own words, Jenny lives each day "to prove to my mother that I was sorry and that I was, after all, worthy of her love" (170).

Bryce Hammond is very much the typical Koontzian hero: an authority figure (a cop, like Tony in *Whispers*) who uses his power wisely and with sensitivity. Indeed, Jenny has never met a man like him: "He had considerable masculine strength and purpose, but he was also capable of tenderness" (271). On the surface he is the strong loving father that an abused child must fantasize about. But in a realistic novel even the most heroic of men have flaws, problems they must overcome during the course of the story, and Bryce's is one of goodness in excess: he takes too much responsibility when things go wrong. As a result, he continues to blame himself for the death of his wife in a car accident that has left his son in a seemingly irreversible coma for the past year.

Significantly, at the outset of this novel both Jenny and Bryce view themselves as villains, as destroyers of families—their children, wives, and fathers. The struggle by Jenny and Bryce to discover the real villains, the real threat to themselves and to the cosmic family of man, is very much what this novel is about. Jenny and Bryce, with young Lisa in tow, embark upon the journey to the heart of darkness that a horror novel promises; and since they have a mainstream realist named Koontz as their author, they will find at the center of that dark heart not only the secret of the evil that threatens them, but also the truth about themselves, a truth that shall set them free.

As he did in *Whispers*, Koontz weaves even minor characters into this thematic structure. Deputy Jake Johnson has been badgered by his domineering father, "Big Ralph," into a profession that Jake despises and is unsuited for. Deputy Tal Whitman's mother was a dope-addict and his father a sociopathic wife-beater "who had shown up once or twice a month merely for the pleasure of slapping his woman senseless and terrorizing his children" (172). Like Hilary Thomas's parents, Tal's also were devoured in their bed of evil by a fire in their Harlem apartment, taking with them Tal's brothers and sisters. But in this novel about disintegrated families, the crucial minor character that is the victim of family violence is the town of Snowfield itself.

Nestled high in the California mountains, Snowfield is the ultimate close-knit, wholesome community, a sort of Mayfield in the Sierras. It is a town where everyone knows everyone else, a cozy and comfortable place, a true "haven from the rude world where violence and unkindness were common" (39), just as a family setting should be. People like and respect each other here; most importantly, they are bonded together by their sense of family. Indeed, Snowfield becomes a metaphor for the cosmic family of man, a network of families which has the potential to live together in peace and mutual respect and dependence.

But into this microcosm of the human family comes an "incredibly violent, unknown enemy" (39) that horribly murders everyone. The loudest sound in Snowfield when Jenny and Lisa arrive is the silence, which Koontz uses stereophonically to produce a remarkably eerie effect. The town is indisputably dead, its metaphorical heart unbeating. And as Jenny goes from house to house, she reacts to the murdered victims—the Karnarskys, Liebermans, and Oxleys—as if they were deceased family members, for in a very real way they are. But now, without its normal network of families, the town has become "utterly alien, a hostile place in which she [Jenny] was an unwelcome stranger" (141). Once again, she and Lisa are without a family. They are about to be joined by Bryce, who is also without a family, and together they will try to fight back the evil and give birth to a new family.

The key to understanding the nature of the evil shape-changer that has attacked Snowfield and now threatens the entire human family lies in understanding its three disciples in the novel. Koontz uses the names of these characters as labels. Stu Wargle is, literally, a man who makes "war" against "girls." Indeed, he twice tries to molest the teen-aged Lisa, once as a man and again as a phantom. Throughout his life, Wargle has been a woman-hater who treats females as servants, lumps of flesh, as "members of another, lesser species" (75). One recalls Koontz's comment about his own father, who "never had any respect for women" (5:23).

Gene Terr, leader of the Demon Chrome, is clearly the "terror" of the human species. No crime against women or children is beyond the pale of this devil-worshiper who would "rather die than take orders from a woman" (296). And so he also carries out unspeakable things to them during Satanic rituals performed by him and his followers of the Demon Chrome. Obviously, the evil shape-changer is quite interested in Gene Terr.

But perhaps "IT's" most promising disciple is Fletcher Kale, who does indeed have all the moral stature of a cabbage, or kale. But "kale" is also a slang term for "money," and certainly it is his lust for wealth, fame, and power which motivates Fletcher's hideous crimes against his family. To take the onomastics one step further, Fletcher's last name, given the right emphasis, could also be pronounced like that of his Hindu namesake, Kali, wife of Shiva. Both Kali and Kale bring death and disease; however, this Kale destroys only man's most precious gifts: wife and child.

The character of Fletcher Kale is a disturbing portrait of contemporary family violence in our society. Hiding beneath a false surface of respectability, Fletcher Kale is a classic example of Hannah Arendt's "banality of evil" (1:12). Evil people, the Israeli philosopher wrote, are not recognizable by their protruding horns or forked tails. Rather, evil is quite ordinary in appearance and hides beneath the meek, bespectacled face of a Nazi administrator like Adolf Eichmann, who truly believed he was merely following orders. In the final analysis, evil is so remarkably banal because it lives inside of each of us, ordinary people, who cannot see the insidious evil we commit every day, whether it be tacitly supporting a cruel war of terrorism against innocent peasants in Nicaragua, allowing an aged parent to wither away alone in a nursing home, or unconsciously belittling wife and child.

Koontz employs Arendt's concept to good effect by at first depicting Kale as an ordinary and upright citizen, as indeed most child and wife abusers are. On the surface, "Fletch" is a tall, good-looking real estate agent who righteously protests his innocence in the shooting of his wife and the mutilation of his son. On the surface, it is merely ordinary chocolate fudge ice cream that he feeds to his wife; she cannot see the overdose of PCP that is about to rip apart her mind. The ordinary seeming Fletcher Kale is in actuality merely one of many men who carry out, while hidden to society like the PCP in the ice cream, "lives of acceptable destruction," (59) hurting those closest to them on a daily basis. With Fletcher Kale, Koontz has taken an all-too-common type of family abuser and simply let him follow those instincts of violence to their logical end: his son Danny's "small, torn, bloody body lying in heap" (61). This is always what *could* happen in an abused family, even one like the young Koontz's, and it is certainly what every abused child fears might happen. Thus, the evil of Fletcher Kale is an all-too-common and ordinary evil. Fletcher Kale is not really a monster; he is us.

And that is the secret of "IT," the evil shape-shifting mass that threatens humankind. As he did with the "undead" in *Whispers*, Koontz again takes a potentially stale device from the horror genre and breathes new life into it. But not before he first *uses* a horror fan's own generic expectations to cleverly manipulate him. Throughout the novel Koontz encourages the reader to believe that the shape-changer is the devil, a combination of Satan, Loki, Minos, and other traditional sources of evil. Of course, this evil rises up from underground, from the Pit, and throughout the book Koontz strategically places references to staring into Hell, voices from Hell, even the "road to Hell." Koontz wants the reader to believe that the creature is the very essence of predestinate evil, one that is "totally inexplicable, beyond reason, pure, complete" (340). However, by the end of *Phantoms*, the hoary concept of a predestined evil from Hell has been turned upon the reader like a mirror, who suddenly finds himself staring rather uncomfortably into his own inexplicable, evil image.

The secret to the shape-changer, which has fed upon humanity for centuries, is that it has merely absorbed all that humanity is—our intelligence, our soul—and owes to us its evolution. The shattering realization which Koontz plants for us at the end of the novel is that the shape-changer's hideous evil is our own. Koontz lets Jenny Paige turn this mirror upon the reader when she says: "If the shape-changer was the Satan of mythology, perhaps the Devil is only a reflection of the savagery and brutality of our own kind. Maybe what we've done is... create the Devil in our own image" (413).

In *Phantoms*, the real devils are human beings, particularly the twisted ones like Kale, Terr, and Wargle, who have never acquired empathy or compassion. To show this, Koontz *uses* family violence, especially the abuse of children, as a metaphor for the human capacity for evil. Evil attacks us at our very core, which is the nuclear family that literally binds us humans together. Evil is *senseless,* which child abuse is because a child cannot hurt anyone. Evil is infinitely malicious, gratifying in a sadistic way, like a cat pawing at a crippled bird, like an adult harming a defenseless child. Indeed, even professional evildoers, prisoners, recognize child abuse as the ultimate evil; Kale must be protected in jail because "in the social classes of prisoners, no one was farther down the ladder than child killers" (260). Gene Terr, the high priest of evil in this novel, knows that family violence, especially child abuse, is the essence of evil. He says to Kale, "You killed your wife. Man, you even killed your own little baby boy. If that isn't HIS [the Devil's] work, then what is?" (396).

Thus, the evil thing which feeds upon Snowfield is merely a distillation of humanity's own evil. It attacks us at our very core—the family. The shape-changer is indeed a phantom, or image that appears only in the mind, something that we create ourselves. And like a phantom, this thing's only reality is the one that we have given it. The shape-changer can be only what it has absorbed from us humans. We are the creators of the phantoms of evil. We are the ones—the Wargles, Terrs, and Kales—that feed upon ourselves and the most innocent among us, the children.

Because she is a child, only Lisa possesses true insight into the evil nature of the shape-changer. She correctly intuits that it has "a web somewhere," and that it sucks the essence from victims and spits out the leftovers like "cherry pits." At a crucial moment, Lisa alerts the others to the shape-changer's spying presence, and it is Lisa who first senses that the shape-changer is finally dead. Why only her? The evil shape-changer is not only a physical presence in Snowfield, but a spiritual one as well. However, only someone with an innocent soul, like Lisa, can sense its spiritual evil. The adults are too crusted over, so imbued with the inherent evil of humanity that the shape-changer is merely a reflection of it.

Lisa's intuition, born of her innocence, also tells her the shape-changer is like God: it is everywhere, seeing all and knowing all. It is her ability to discern the similarity between the devilish shape-changer and God that provides the key to understanding the metaphysics of good and evil in this novel. If the devilish shape-changer is a reflection of the ultimate evil in us, then the reverse must also be true: God must be a reflection of the ultimate good in us: our courage, sympathy, and compassion. If humans are the creators of evil, then we are also the creators of good. If "Hell is where we make it," (413) then so is Heaven.

Thus, the real battle in *Phantoms* is between the good and evil in man. Snowfield, symbolic of the cosmic family of man, has been invaded by an evil brought upon man by himself. And now the family of man, of whom Jenny is the matriarch and Bryce the patriarch, must come together and draw upon the eternal human verities of hope, pity, courage, compassion, and sacrifice to fight back the evil and to reunite the disintegrated family. It is as if Koontz wanted to confront these characters with the worst thing imaginable, to strip human beings of everything important, especially the bonds of family, and to see what was there. He found not only the evil that has always plagued us, but also a resilience and nobility that are our true selves, our race's true glory. The ability to come together into these units called families is what keeps us going, what saves us. The ultimate image in this novel of families is of Bryce, Jenny, and Tal standing in a circle around young Lisa as they make their last stand against the evil shape-changer. This is humanity's last stand, too, and it is won by people who are able to find the good in each other and to bond together into a fighting unit known as family.

The battle in Snowfield is won, but not the war. As is sometimes the vogue, there is a false ending in *Phantoms*: a last, unexpected upsurge of evil, which was thought destroyed, surprises the survivors of Snowfield, two of whom are recuperating in the hospital. Although the surprise attack by Kale and Terr is a clichéd device, it can be justified as part of the novel's statement that we must be ever vigilant against this form of evil, that it can invade us in even the most ordinary and safest of havens—a hospital.

The ultimate ending is also a beginning for families. Bryce, Jenny, and Lisa come together as a new family. There is hope that the comatose Timmy will soon join them. Tal marries Paula and another family begins. Most importantly, a belief in Heaven and in the transcendent purpose God gives to our lives is Joyously reaffirmed.

Thus, the ending of *Phantoms*, as well as of *Whispers*, is in an important way a throwback to much of premodern horror literature, where the destructive side of horror was often downplayed in the favor of the reconstructive. For example, in S. Fowler Wright's *Dawn* (1929), which like *Phantoms* is a novel of catastrophe, most of Great Britain drowns when the island slips into the sea, yet the emphasis at the end is on the hope of building a new world. At the end of *Phantoms* an entire town has been wiped out, yet the emphasis is on the hope for humankind that is implicit in the joyful rebirth of families.

3. NOVELS OF TRANSCENDENCE

In *Whispers*, the intimate relationship that bonds a man and a woman together also lifts them above their sordid and haunting pasts, sustaining them in their battle against a brutality born of child abuse. In *Phantoms*, a group of individuals, each reeling from the violence and abuse that have torn apart their families, bonds together to form a new family in order to overcome the evil that is an unfortunate part of human nature. And if *Phantoms* is a sequel to *Whispers*, then *Strangers* completes the trilogy. Through contact with the advanced alien culture and its miraculous gifts, there is hope that the bonding between couples and families in *Phantoms* and *Whispers* can be extended and will "soon exist between all men and women" (3:680) of the human race. Perhaps

110

humankind will finally be able to look beyond itself, and in so doing be joyously transformed.

Koontz had even gently teased his readers with advance notice of the transcendence of *Strangers,* when he wrote in the last sentence of *Phantoms:* "What mysteries and miracles, what horrors and joys were being ground out at this very moment, to be served up in times to come?" (425). Three years later, with the publication of *Strangers,* we found out what Koontz had been grinding out and preparing to serve up: his most ambitious novel to date, and one that builds upon his technique of blending mainstream elements with the conventions of the horror/suspense novel, a technique which he had employed so successfully in *Whispers* and *Phantoms.*

All three novels use the trappings of the horror/suspense novel merely as background and as an occasion for the characters' search for answers to basic questions about human existence: who are we? How do we find meaning in our lives? How does the past influence our present and future selves? What does it mean to love another? Are man and the universe basically good or evil? These are the existential questions of the loose trilogy formed by *Whispers, Phantoms,* and *Strangers.* Answers to the questions are provided on three levels: the couple, the nuclear family, the human family. Alone, Koontz seems to be saying, humans are nothing. We need each other as lovers, as families, as a species. And he wrote three novels to prove it.

Although the three works have been praised, and rightfully so, for being exciting and "fun" reads, it's clear that at the same time Koontz is also using the horror/suspense novel as a vehicle for another purpose. One of his comments about the mainstream techniques of *Strangers* applies equally as well to *Whispers* and *Phantoms.* Koontz said that he consciously attempted "to write a thriller that transcended the genre...I wanted not only to thrill and spook, but to engender a really overwhelming sense of mystery, wonder, awe, and a sense of pride and excitement in the whole damn human race" (5:24).

Judging from the critical reception, Koontz was successful in transcending the limitations of genre in *Strangers.* Its finely drawn characterizations, elaborate interweaving of plot and theme, speculative materials, and masterful use of suspense make *Strangers* a *sui generis:* a unique blend of the best elements of genre writing and mainstream realism. However, it is difficult to imagine Koontz achieving this important breakthrough without having first written two earlier novels, *Whispers* and *Phantoms,* which also attempted the same blend, and which achieved, in their own way, a similar transcendence, both thematically and artistically.

VIII.

DARK GENESIS:

WATCHERS AND *SHADOWFIRES*

BY STAN BROOKS

"I'm being guided by the belief that a thriller does not have to be just thrilling or just scary but can also be at times funny, touching, melancholy, uplifting, and even intellectually exhilarating."
—Dean Koontz (1)

Koontz's horrors do not necessarily come from the dark shadows of some supernatural neverworld, nor must they arrive in a gleaming, phallic-shaped alien spacecraft. Koontz horrors are the result of good old-fashioned Yankee ingenuity. And perhaps there's something even more supernatural in the fact that mankind—the same species that brought the world the Hula-hoop, Superglue and Spam—has also developed Napalm, Cruise Missiles, and killer bacteria. And it is this notion that supplies hammer and nails for the framework of both *Watchers* and *Shadowfires*. With these tools, Koontz has constructed two novels of twisted technology. Both contain genetic nightmares; and *Watchers*, a genetically engineered hope for all humankind.

This hope takes the form of a Golden Retriever who is more than he, at first, seems. Named Einstein by his newfound friend (he rejects the term master), Travis Cornell, he is the result of an experiment in genetic engineering: a dog as intelligent as man. He is, arguably, Koontz's most likable, unusual character to date. Although he's not the first intelligent canine to wag its tail through a Koontz novel.

He introduced Brutus in his 1973 novel, *The Haunted Earth*. Brutus was a hell-hound, a former human being who has kept his human intelligence and perspectives, and there lies the wonderful difference.

Einstein sees the world through a unique perspective. For although he possesses human intelligence, he is still very much a dog.

112

He has his own world-view, which makes for some interesting observations. And unlike Brutus, Einstein is a true innocent. Everything he sees brings wonderment. He is like a child eagerly discovering the mysteries of the universe. And just as a parent has his world given new life, new meaning, through the unspoiled eyes of his children, a desperate, depressed Travis Cornell, and a confused, timid Nora Devon, see new hope, new life through the noble eyes of a Golden Retriever. And through meeting Einstein, their lives are made complete and given purpose. He gives them hope. Dignity. And this becomes a recurring theme in *Watchers*. Humankind can resurface from the murky depths of despair and find self-worth and hope. For if man can create a creature like Einstein, if he can mirror the image of his own intellect in another species, then he has attained the spirit of God. How can that not give all humankind hope?

> What miracle could bring more joy, more respect for the mysteries of nature, more sheer exhuberance over the unanticipated wonders of life? Somehow, in the very idea of the dog's personality and human intelligence combined in a single creature, one had a hope of a species at once as gifted as humankind but more noble and worthy. And what fantasy of adults was more common than that, one day, another intelligent species would be found to share the vast, cold universe and, by sharing it, would at last provide some relief from our race's unspeakable loneliness and sense of quiet desperation? (2:302)

Before Einstein entered his life, Travis was being pulled down into an ocean of depression. Tragedy after tragedy had befallen Travis, and those he cared about. His life was devoid of hope. He had entered self-imposed emotional exile to spare himself, and others, further tragedy.

For Travis Cornell, Einstein is not just a super-intelligent canine with military potential, but a living life raft. It is as though he were sent from God to show Travis that he had not lost his ability to love.

> The retriever's friskiness and the frenzied wagging of its tail had an unexpected effect on Travis. For a long time his mind had been in a dark place, filled with thoughts of death, culminating in today's journey. But this animal's unadulterated joy in being alive was like a spotlight that pierced Travis's inner gloom and reminded him that life had a brighter side from which he had long turned away. (2:21)

And as that love resurfaces, both he and Einstein soon find they have enough to share. The dog becomes the catalyst that brings Nora Devon and Travis together.

Nora, like Einstein, is an innocent. She has lived a sheltered life under the rule of her deranged Aunt Violet. With the death of her aunt, for the first time she must face the outside world—a world alien to her. Nora's world has been that available to her only through books and paintings. And because she is innocent, because—as her aunt used to say—she is the mouse in a world of cats, she soon finds herself preyed upon. Like Travis, Nora lives in emotional exile. Nora's life with her crazed aunt has left deep social scars. She is convinced that she is undesirable, homely, even ugly. She has also been taught that people, especially men, are evil and will do her harm. And although the old woman has been dead for a year, Nora still lives in her house surrounded by her possessions, her memory. At a point when Nora begins to believe that her aunt may have been wrong, the cat enters in the form of a TV repairman.

Art Streck is the first major stumbling block in Nora's resocialization. He is a cocky, overbearing, sadistic man who accurately perceives Nora as an easy target for his perverse pleasures. Although Streck's character enters the novel, terrorizes Nora, and departs, not to be heard from again, all within twenty-five pages, he holds an important role in the story. He helps us to better understand Nora Devon. He shows us that the harm done her by Aunt Violet cuts deep into her personality. After seeing the interaction between Art Streck and Nora Devon, it is difficult not to behold even a minute strengthening of her character as anything less than a miracle.

Koontz knows that human perseverance can result in miracles. His own rise to best-selling author is a miracle of sorts. He was the victim of psychological and physical abuse as a child. He purged himself of the dark shadow of that abuse, that betrayal by his alcoholic father, through the writing of *Whispers*. And his more recent works, *Watchers* no exception, have a more hopeful feel to them. Nora Devon finds the key to free the strength she possesses, the strength locked inside for so long. And that key is love.

There is, of course, a dark side to human nature. That dark side is embodied in Koontz's characterization of Vince Nasco. Vince Nasco is also trying to better himself. He's trying his best to achieve a Godlike state—immortality, an immortality gained by sucking the life from his victims and using this energy to revitalize his own soul. It is his belief that with each person he kills he gets closer to his goal. He also seems to believe the more sadistic the killings, the greater the life force he is able to absorb. He feels recharged through the agony of others.

> He wanted her to be cooperative until he could tie
> her up and deal with her at a more leisurely pace.
> The two shootings had been satisfying, but he wanted
> to draw this one out, kill her more slowly. Some-
> times, death could be savored like good food, fine
> wine, and glorious sunsets. (2:41)

Nasco knows he is very close to immortality. He sees in Einstein an opportunity to become rich as well. He plans to ransom the
dog to the highest bidder, killing Travis and Nora in the bargain. It is
the character of Nasco that adds suspense to the novel. There is another
that brings us the horror.

Einstein was not the only product of genetic research to come
out of the Frances Project; there was the creature known as The Outsider.

The Outsider is, at once, horrific and pathetic—deserving of
equal doses of fear and pity. Like Einstein, it is a creation of man.
Unlike Einstein, it cannot be identified with any known species. It is
the ultimate outcast, a monster.

Yet it possesses intellect. Intellect is a uniquely human capacity, and it may not be given to another creature without that creature
developing some human characteristics. Even the Outsider can understand beauty. It can feel jealousy. It can hate. It kills out of self-ha-
tred and anger at humankind for having created it in such a demonic
image.

In some ways Koontz's Outsider is akin to Mary Shelley's
Frankenstein monster. Both creatures were shunned by their creators.
Both were marked as outcasts, the only of their kind to exist. Finally,
both were capable of the vilest of deeds, yet they were creatures to be
pitied. They are painfully aware of their own ugliness.

> "I had admired the perfect forms of my cot-
> tagers—their grace, beauty, and delicate complexions;
> but how was I terrified when I viewed myself in a
> transparent pool! At first I stared back, unable to be-
> lieve that it was indeed I who was reflected in the mir-
> ror; and when I became fully convinced that I was in
> reality the monster that I am, I was filled with the
> bitterest of sensations of despondence and mortifica-
> tion." (3:98)

The Outsider huddled there, Lea thought, trying
to take heart from its meager treasures, trying to make
as much of a home for itself as was possible. Once in
a while it picked up this jagged shard from a mirror
and stared at itself, perhaps searching hopefully for an

aspect of its countenance that was not ugly, perhaps trying to come to terms with what it was. And failing. Surely failing. (2:197)

For the Frankenstein monster and The Outsider, release from torment can only be obtained through death. Death is the conclusion of their nightmare.

For Dr. Eric Leben of Leigh Nichols's *Shadowfires*, death is the genesis of the nightmare.

In this, his final Leigh Nichols novel, Koontz has reshaped his fascination with defeating death into a dark, and at times, grotesquely humorous tale, written in the horrific style of his earlier *Darkfall* and *Phantoms*.

As a novel of fear, it too embraces the Frankenstein Monster creation theme and takes it several steps further: a creation which is the product of its own creator's dead viscera, muscle, and bone; a creature so horrible it cannot comprehend even the slightest compassion allowed Mary Shelley's modern Prometheus: a melancholy vision of a science that seeks to cheat death, thereby assuming the insolence of a God.

> "No, My God, what have I made of myself?" he wondered, nausea twisting his belly. I'm both researcher and subject. Creator and creation, and that has to've been a mistake, a terrible mistake. Could I have become...my own Frankenstein Monster? (4:174)

> Genetic Chaos, Whit had said. Devolution. Moments ago those words had meant little or nothing to Ben. Now, on his first glimpse of the thing Eric Leben had become, he understood as much as he needed to understand for the moment. Leben was both Dr. Frankenstein and the Frankenstein Monster, both the experimenter and the experiment, a genius and a damned soul. (4:414)

Indeed, Dr. Eric Leben has become his own Frankenstein Monster, a monster created through genetic tampering in a surreptitious attempt at immortality. In this case, not immortality to continue experiencing the joys and wonders of life, but rather, immortality to avoid the damnation certain with death—of becoming a slave to the shadowfires of hell. For this is Eric's destiny. He's a person, unlike Travis and Nora, who cannot call upon human perseverance to crawl from the dark waters of despair and depression. He's the antithesis of Koontz's own optimistic outlook. He is a man gifted with brilliance and wealth, but impoverished in the emotion that gives strength to many of

Koontz's characters—he's unable to feel love. A personality defect nurtured within him—*à la* vintage Koontz—by an unthinkably deranged childhood.

He had repeatedly been the victim of his perverse Uncle Hampstead's sexual abuse, an abuse that he ended himself at the impressionable age of nine with the help of a butcher's knife, sending his uncle to his eternal damnation.

> In spite of all his education, in spite of his ability
> to reason, he was illogical about this one thing: in his
> heart he believed that he would go to hell when he
> died, not merely because he had sinned with his uncle,
> but because he had killed his uncle as well, and was
> both a fornicator and a murderer. (4:262)

This notion has been drilled deep into Eric's young mind by his maniacally religious, overzealous parents who had prayed over the boy for hours at a time in an attempt to redeem his lost soul.

Koontz has created in Leben a character who is a genius in the science of recombinant DNA and genetic research, a man whose science is based upon logic and a belief in heredity, encompassed in the wider belief of Darwinian evolution. The belief in evolution is in direct conflict with the belief in creation, and would seem to be in conflict with the belief in God. Why then, would Koontz have Leben fear so for his soul? If there is no God, there is certainly no heaven, no hell. Leben's dilemma cannot be addressed by traditional theologies. For Dr. Eric Leben, through his own intellectual process, and not merely taking verbatim the teachings of someone else, has developed his own theology, a theology which embraces both scientific fact and spiritualistic faith, a theology, a portion of which, is shared by Leben's literary creator.

> I believe that within ourselves we can see a moral
> imperative that cannot be explained by the view of hu-
> mankind as a simple product of Darwinian evolution:
> Our overwhelming need to love and be loved, our
> willingness to sacrifice ourselves for close friends and
> loved ones, can be accepted as a survival instinct only
> by the most tortured paths of reason (I've heard them
> all), for in fact love and self-sacrifice are qualities
> that, by Darwinian theory, would have been bred out
> of us as counterproductive if we were simply the
> products of a mechanical process of evolution un-
> touched by the hand of God. Now don't get me
> wrong: I believe we are evolved creatures and that we
> probably did follow the path up from crawling fish to
> ape to man; but I just don't think that is the whole

story. Beyond evolution there is a guiding consciousness, and I know it as surely as I know that I need
food to go on living. (5)

If there is a guiding consciousness to love and self-sacrifice,
there must be another, evil consciousness to hate and sacrifice others.
It is the latter which drives the Leben-thing on after Eric's accident.
For the monster he has made of himself is not a creation of God and
does not live by his rules. Eric has ceased to exist, despite his wildcard
experiment, when that garbage truck strikes him, smashing in his skull.
He has not discovered a way to defeat death; he has merely devised a
means of donating his body to other, darker forms of life. And it is this
imperative which Koontz wants us to understand. It is an imperative
that Leben realizes himself—albeit too late—in a moment of black humor.

Suddenly the situation seemed uproariously funny
to Eric: a dead man sitting at breakfast, chomping
Farmer John sausages, pouring hot Maxwell House
down his cold gullet, desperately trying to be one of
the living, as if death could be reversed by pretense,
as if life could be regained merely by the performance
of enough mundane activities—showering, brushing
his teeth, eating, drinking, crapping—and by the con-
sumption of enough homely products. He must be
alive, because they wouldn't have Farmer John
sausages and Maxwell House in either heaven or hell.
Would they? He must be alive because he had used
his Mr. Coffee machine and his electric oven, and
over in the corner his Westinghouse refrigerator was
humming softly, and although those manufacturers'
wares were widely distributed, surely none of them
would be found on the far shores of the river Styx, so
he must be alive. (4:169)

But of course he is only fooling himself. What he has become
is a being of high-tech science. And although he is, by appearances,
more terrifying, he is not the only such creature in *Shadowfires*. There
is another in the novel who is both creator and creation, another
damned soul—Anson Sharp.

Sharp is a Vietnam veteran and a disgrace to the men he has
served with: a black marketeer and ultimately a murderer, under Ben
Shadway's command, who by eliminating incriminating witnesses,
managed to escape further punishment beyond the loss of his stripes and
dishonorable discharge.

118

He later becomes an expert computer programmer and hacker, landing a job at TRW, which enables him to electronically alter his military records: the dishonorable discharge becomes honorable, an enlistment becomes a full commission, and he even sees fit to add a few commendations. By creating the "new and improved" Anson Sharp, he is accepted into the Defense Security Agency training program. Once there, he returns to murder as a means of eliminating rivals and quickly climbs the ladder to the status of Deputy Director. So while Anson Sharp may not present as horrifying a visage as Eric Leben, he is every bit as horrible.

> No cadaver could be found in the house, neither Sarah Kiel's nor anybody else's, and Sharp was disappointed. The nude and crucified blonde in Placentia had been unexpected and kinky, a welcome change from the corpses he usually saw. Victims of guns, knives, plastique, and garroting wire were old news to Sharp; he had seen them in such plentitude over the years that he no longer got a kick out of them. But he had sure gotten a kick out of that bimbo nailed to the wall, and he was curious to see what Leben's deranged and rotting mind might come up with next. (4:139)

Criminal minds in high government positions. It is an idea, a horror, that has entered Koontz novels before: network chief George Alexander in *The Eyes of Darkness*, the Army's Col. Falkirk in *Strangers*. In an age of electronic information, where orders can be carried out seconds after being issued—without verification—where millions of dollars can change hands across the globe by a push of a button, it is easy to imagine the potential for destruction should such evil men achieve unchecked governmental power. We've seen it—all too recently—with Watergate, Abscam, and the ill-conceived Iranian arms deal. Men such as these exist, they are not merely the fantasy of Dean Koontz. And this is why such men as Anson Sharp are more terrifying than the Frankenstein Monster—they exist by God, *they exist!*

Unfortunately, the Koontz optimism that guides such characters' fates does not always reveal itself in the real world. But a Koontz novel is an escape from the real world. And there is always the light at the end, the real means to immortality.

> Drifting down into a restful darkness, Ben almost felt sorry for Eric Leben, because the scientist had never realized love was the closest thing to immortality that man could ever know and that the only—and best—answer to death was loving. Loving. (4:143)

119

IX.

THE THREE FACES OF EVIL:

THE MONSTERS OF *WHISPERS*, *PHANTOMS*, AND *DARKFALL*

BY MICHAEL A. MORRISON

The zombie. The maniac. The demon. Gigantic wasps, crabs, spiders. Voodoo priests. Monsters all, such figures of evil leer out at us from the pages of countless horror tales and flicker across screens where numberless genre films unreel. These creatures embody one of the central preoccupations of horror fiction: the representation and delineation of evil. What is Evil? What is its source? Is Evil innate in man? Is it the Devil's doing? Or is it a cosmic, disembodied power, the incarnation of uncaring—or worse, inimical—gods that rule the universe? The monster vivifies these anxieties and looms large in tales of horror, fantasy, and science fiction.

And so it does in mainstream thrillers such as the novels of Dean Koontz. In three successive novels—*Whispers* (1980), *Phantoms* (1983), and *Darkfall* (1984)—Koontz uses a familiar figure of the monstrous to posit three quite different views of the nature of Evil. And, particularly in the first two, he plays upon the expectations we readers of horror fiction bring to these novels, implicitly criticizing conventional monsters of the genre as inadequate avatars of Evil for the modern world.

120

1.

ICONS OF THE LIVING DEAD:
THE TWINNING OF BRUNO FRYE

I just wish all of the villains in this piece were thoroughly vile and despicable.
It seems wrong, somehow, to feel so much sympathy for them.
—Joshua Rhinehart in *Whispers*

At first, *Whispers* seems a simple genre novel of the psycho-pathic-madman-assaults-woman variety. Hilary Thomas, a beautiful, successful Hollywood screenwriter, becomes the object of the unwanted attentions of Bruno Frye, whom she thinks is merely a California wine merchant. Indeed, her only prior encounter with Frye was at his Napa Valley vineyard, which she visited while researching a screenplay. But at times Bruno plunges into madness, and, for reasons unknown, he comes after Hilary with a knife.

But gradually, *Whispers* emerges as more subtle and complex than it initially appears. In the guise of a thriller, Koontz's novel uses such traditional icons of horror fiction as the maniac, the zombie, and the demon to develop a surprisingly liberal notion of the nature and source of the evil, the mindless violence, that seems to define late twentieth-century America.

Describing Frye's first attack, Koontz paints a quintessential portrait of the maniac. Raging toward Hilary "like a demon leaping out of a crack in hell" (35), Frye is an elemental image of the monstrous in man:

> His demeanor was that of a lunatic. His eyes flashed, not icy as they had been, but watery and hot, fevered. Sweat streamed down his face. His lips worked ceaselessly, even though he was not speaking; they writhed and twisted, pulled back over his teeth, then pushed out in a childish pout, forming a sneer, then a weird little smile, then a fierce scowl, then an expression for which there was no name. (33-34)

Frye's attack is overtly sexual—his chosen weapon is, after all, a knife. But Hilary is not one to let a slavering madman rape and murder her without a fight. Arming herself with a pistol, she confronts her attacker. She shoots at him twice, first shattering his knife, then hitting him. Frye goes down.

At which point Koontz introduces (implicitly) the image of the zombie, the walking dead. His description of the aftermath of Frye's shooting prefigures what is to come.

> She sighed and lowered the pistol.
> Dead. He was dead.
> She had killed a man.
> Dreading the coming ordeal with police and reports, she edged around the outstretched arm and headed for the hall door.
> Suddenly, he was not dead anymore. (37)

Merely wounded, Frye comes at Hilary again. This first attack is a paradigm of his role in the rest of the novel: for the next 400 pages, neither we nor Koontz's characters are sure whether he is dead.

Hilary ends Frye's second assault by planting her .32 automatic securely on his scrotum and making the obvious threat. But the madman escapes. Sensing that she couldn't kill even him in cold blood, he just walks out.

Hilary Thomas and Bruno Frye, heroine and villain, comprise a study in parallels and contrasts. Both are adults living in the shadow of childhood. Both are victims of parental abuse, and both carry deep-seated neuroses as a consequence. Indeed, all the main figures of Koontz's novel reflect the constricting influences of childhood on adult life—the sins of the fathers and mothers. This theme is vivified even in the personalities of less neurotic characters, such as the novel's hero Tony Clemenza, the Los Angeles cop who becomes Hilary's companion, protector, and lover.

To Hilary, at the pinnacle of success in her chosen field, life seems a little unreal, a "fantasy, a marvelous fairytale" (9). Bright, talented, and self-reliant, she is also deeply insecure: for her, "the world was a dangerous place, a shadowy cellar with nightmare creatures crouching in the dark corners" (43). As events will show, she is not far wrong: in the world of *Whispers* violence and horror descend on innocents with the capriciousness of a tornado. It is the world of Hollywood, of California in the '80s, a world whose moral underpinnings are no more stable than its earthquake-ridden landscape.

Hilary's quiet paranoia stems from her childhood in Chicago: a nightmare of abuse at the hands of her violent, alcoholic father Earl and her uncaring mother Emma. She emerged from those years terrified of emotional commitment, emotionally hamstrung by hatred of her parents, and plagued by unconscious guilt over her father, whom she knifed to death in self-defense. So, to repress her memories and salve her psychic wounds, Hilary has become a recluse and workaholic. Her operant myth is that there exists a level of success that will truly free her, that will provide sufficient security for her to "cast out the demons—my parents, Chicago, all those bad memories" (24). But it will be not her work but rather the "crouching nightmare" (20) of Bruno Frye that enables her to conquer her fears and her past.

Yet, if Hilary is seriously neurotic, Bruno Frye is in never-never land. The Napa Valley vintner can pass for human: various characters perceive him as "an important and successful man" (27) and "a leading figure in the community" (190). But Koontz portrays him as a human monster. He is a great bull of a man, immensely powerful and awesomely voracious. Celebrating violence and sadism, consumed by blood lust and rage, Frye comes at us "like an elemental force" (118).

But amidst the sound and fury of Frye's first attacks on Hilary, Koontz drops a clue that this man/monster is more than your garden variety psychopath. Horrifying nightmares and hallucinations plague Bruno—dreams of whispers:

> [The nightmare] would come to him now as it always did when he slept, as it had all his life, and he would wake with a scream caught in the back of his throat. As always, he would not be able to recall what the dream had been about. But upon waking, he would hear the whispers, the loud but unintelligible whispers, and he would feel something moving on his body, all over his body, on his face, trying to get into his mouth and nose, some horrible *thing*. (312)

Horrible indeed. As we will learn, Bruno's dreams are the key to his psychosis, a fearsome remembrance of abuses past.

As Koontz leads us deeper into Bruno's dementia, he reveals the delusion that drives it: Frye believes that Hilary is his mother reincarnate. Indeed, it is Hilary's chance resemblance to Bruno's long-dead mother Katherine, which he happened to notice during her visit to his vineyard, that determines him to kill her. She is, in fact, the twenty-fourth woman to fall victim to this phantasm.

With the introduction of Frye's delusion, Koontz explicitly invokes another icon of the living dead: the vampire. Bruno believes *literally* that Hilary is one of "the living dead," that she is "his mother come back from the grave," and that only through ritual can he "cancel out her supernatural powers of regeneration" (96). His rituals and their implements derive explicitly from the post-Bram Stoker vampire tale. (At one point, Koontz shows an attendant at the city morgue reading "a few chapters of a really good Stephen King novel about vampires on the loose in New England" [176].) Frye carries in his gray Dodge van the accoutrements of the folkloric vampire killer (linen bags of garlic, wooden stakes, etc.), and his fantasies of Hilary's slaughter exude images from vampire fiction and film:

> Cut out her heart. Pound a wooden stake through
> it. Cut off her head. Fill her mouth with garlic. He
> also intended to take the head and the heart with him
> when he left the house; he would bury the pair of
> grisly trophies in separate and secret graves, in the
> hallowed ground of two different churchyards, and far
> away from wherever the body itself might be interred.
> (118)

We know, of course, that Hilary is neither vampire nor Katherine reincarnate, and are thus aware from the start that Koontz is making unconventional use of genre symbols of evil—in *Whispers*, of the living dead. In addition to the imagined vampire, he will soon introduce a zombie that is not undead, and a schizophrenic (the maniac) that is far more complex than Jekyll and Hyde.

Following Frye's escape, the police appear. Detective Tony Clemenza and his partner Frank Howard interrupt their hunt for a pusher and rapist named Bobby "Angel" Valdez to look into Hilary's case. Faced with overwhelming evidence of Frye's innocence, they are skeptical—until Frye attacks again. This time, Hilary kills him.

As if to assuage any doubt that Frye is indisputably dead, Koontz takes us and Hilary to the morgue. The corpse has Frye's ID, but Hilary doesn't need to identify the distinctive carcass of her assailant. Yet, even in this scene, Koontz foreshadows what is to come, invoking an image from a hundred zombie and vampire movies. Looking at Frye's corpse, Hilary has "the insane feeling that any moment he would turn his head towards her and open his eyes." Then "another absurd but chilling thought struck her: "What if [the corpse] sits up on the cart and throws the sheet off?" (148). Nothing of the sort happens, though, and Hilary leaves "thoroughly relieved and even delighted that [Frye] was dead" (148).

We are now 150 pages into a 502-page book. Frye is dead. Hilary is safe. And we are wondering what the devil Koontz is up to. His several subplots—the stress applied to Tony's and Frank's partnership by Frank's cynicism and bitterness, the budding romance between Hilary and Tony, the search for Bobby Valdez—seem inadequate to sustain several hundred more pages. And as these subplots unfold, we watch the journey of the corpse of Bruno Frye through embalmment and burial in short, strangely ominous scenes that give no clue that he is not well and truly defunct.

Our first hints that the creature may still be among us are subtle ones: Hilary receives voiceless telephone calls; Frye's coffin is violated by parties unknown; Joshua Rhinehart, the executor of the Frye estate, senses "an evil presence in the darkness, a thing crouching and waiting" (334) as he leaves the funeral home where Bruno lies in state. Implanted like seeds in the latter chapters of Part I ("The Living and the

Dead"), these incidents will bear fruit in Part II ("The Living and the Living Dead"), when Bruno returns.

But just before this happens, Joshua Rhinehart suffers a dream. Dreams in Koontz's novels are fraught with meaning, and this one is no exception:

> In the nightmare, several dead men—all of them duplicates of Bruno Frye—had risen up from their caskets and from the porcelain and stainless steel embalming tables; [Joshua] had run into the night...but they had come after him, had searched the shadows for him, moving jerkily, calling his name in their flat, dead voices (216).

In this dream, which reads like an out-take from *Night of the Living Dead*, Koontz foreshadows Bruno's return and embeds clues as to his true nature.

But now Frye is back. Like a primal force of nature, he again attacks Hilary. Confronted with what appears unarguably to be a "walking dead man," she is almost as troubled by the implied subversion of reality as by the immediate threat:

> As she watched Bruno Frye coming through the archway, Hilary thought she must be losing her mind. The man was dead. Dead! She had stabbed him twice, had seen his blood. She had seen him in the morgue, too, cold and yellow-gray and lifeless. An autopsy had been performed. A death certificate had been signed. *Dead men don't walk.* Nevertheless, he was back from the grave.... (269)

Bruno's return, "pasty-faced, shaking violently, obviously on the edge of hysteria," propels us into Part II, where Koontz's thriller turns into a mystery.

This change in the narrative structure of *Whispers* occurs as Hilary, her policeman lover Tony, and the Frye's lawyer Joshua Rhinehart dig into the history of the Frye family. Impelled almost as much by curiosity as by their desire to protect Hilary, they probe back in time: first into the recent past of Frye's autopsy, embalming, and burial; then further back into his adult life and relationships; and ultimately, in an interview with Rita Yancy, the prostitute who was midwife at Bruno's birth, into the dark history of the family Frye. Their search for the truth of Bruno Frye—"Was the impossible possible? Could a dead man walk?" (283)—plunges them (and us) into a bewildering maelstrom of modern evil.

THE THREE FACES OF EVIL, BY MICHAEL A. MORRISON

As Part II unfolds, the traditional, simplistic evil figures of the maniac and the zombie give way to a complex psychological portrait of a tortured victim. From the beginning of their quest, Hilary, Tony, and Joshua have thought of Frye as "the most evil, vicious sort of monster," as "the Beast from Hell [that] walks among us in the clothes of a common man" (377). But as the community of truth-seekers penetrates the web of lies and half-truths that enmeshes the figure of Bruno Frye, their (and our) identification of him as the provenance of evil becomes as murky as the swamp of dementia and perversion that is the Frye family history.

For Hilary, Tony, and Joshua have discovered a fundamental principle of the world of *Whispers*: that truth is as unstable as the fault-ridden earth beneath their feet. Piecing together clues, rumors, and speculation, they consider several solutions to the mystery of Bruno's return, only to have to jettison each. What deflects them from the truth is the unreliability of public myth, of "common knowledge," about Frye's past: he was an only child; Katherine adopted him; she had no natural children, etc. All these stories are found to be wrong. So, in the face of such unreliable knowledge, speculations abound: Frye wasn't really killed; Frye has, in fact, returned from the dead; Frye had a brother; Frye had hired a lookalike. Although none of these explanations proves correct either, each moves the figure of the monster farther from the traditional generic embodiment of evil, and takes us closer to the ambiguous heart of evil in the novel. Like petals on a diseased flower, the layers of the Frye family history unfold to expose a legacy of madness and abuse.

Finally, from the midwife at Bruno's birth, prostitute Rita Yancy, the searchers learn the answer: Bruno is neither zombie nor supernatural creature; rather, he is the pathetic victim of his psychotic mother Katherine. From Rita they also learn that Bruno had a twin. In Katherine's story, as recounted by Yancy, Koontz introduces a third genre icon: the demon. Katherine's delusion, which she passed on to the son she bore, Bruno Frye, and to his twin brother, was that she had been "raped by a thing from hell, a green scaly thing with huge eyes and a forked tongue and long claws" (459). Like the figure of Hilary-as-vampire in the mind of her son, Katherine's demon lover exists only in her mind. But it was a delusion she needed desperately, and to preserve it Katherine lived the pretense that she was raising but a single child, the son of a friend. To this end she "gave the boys just one name. She allowed only one of them to go out in public at one time. She forced them to live one life" (469). Thus was born Bruno's dementia. In the psychic pressure cooker of his mother's madness—and under the threat of her truly monstrous punishment, which now haunts his dreams—Bruno and his brother came to believe her "demon fantasy," accepting at the deepest levels of their minds that they were but a single person: "two individuals with one personality, one self-aware-ness, one self-image" (470).

Thus is the figure of the monster in *Whispers* transformed into a victim. In the pantheon of horror, Bruno Frye is a variant on the split personality, the Jekyll/Hyde symbol of human duality. To be sure, Bruno—each Bruno—is truly schizophrenic. Appearing normal in society, he harbors a hidden self, "the demon half of his personality" (381), that rages to the surface in the (imagined) presence of Katherine's reincarnated spirit. Koontz's clever variation is that Frye's personality has undergone both fission and fusion; he is both himself and his brother. But now

> ...himself was dead.... For forty years, he had posed as an ordinary man, and he had passed for normal with considerable success. But he could not do that any more. Half of him was dead.... Without himself to turn to, without his other self to give advice and offer suggestions, he did not have the resources to maintain the charade. (413)

The grotesque figure of Bruno Frye—a meld of the motifs of the dual personality, the *doppelgänger*, and the monstrous twin—ranks with Niles Perry in Thomas Tryon's *The Other* (1971) as one of the most original psychological aberrations in horror fiction. For the characters in the novel and for us Bruno remains monstrous and malignant, but not evil—at least not in a traditional sense.

Is then Katherine the progenitor of evil in the uncertain world of this novel? No sooner does the question occur to Hilary and her compatriots when up from the swamp of the Frye family history bubbles yet another awful horror. It is Leo, the insanely egomaniacal, ruthlessly autocratic patriarch of the Fryes, who had brutalized, sexually abused, and finally impregnated his daughter Katherine. This truth leaves the wretched figure of Bruno's mother, frantically trying to preserve her public image of "a saintly woman who took in a poor foundling" (399), too pathetic and tragic a figure to serve as the wellspring of evil. The history of horror stops at Leo, but we are left uncertain as to the nature and source of evil. Indeed, evil itself seems to have gotten lost in the rack of victims that is the family tree of Bruno Frye.

Bruno Frye, at once monster and victim, berserker and figure of pathos, reminds us of our own dual natures—of the beasts within us all—and of how childhood traumas and terrors can shape our dreams and waking lives. But Bruno also symbolizes the motiveless malignity that surrounds us. And the transformation of his iconographic function in Koontz's novel—from traditionally evil maniac to simplistically evil zombie to psychologically complex victim—suggests that the source of evil is neither supernatural agency nor individual, but rather society. This evolution of the figure of the monster inverts and revises the traditional genre motifs Koontz has invoked and emphasizes their inefficacy as symbols of evil for the modern world. With his next novel, *Phantoms*, Koontz will use another collection of horror icons to propound a quite different view of evil.

2.

IN HIS IMAGE:
THE DEVIL ON A GLASS SLIDE

There's no use wasting energy being afraid of devils, demons and things that go bump in the night...because, ultimately, we'll never encounter anything more terrifying than the monsters among us. Hell is where we make it.
— Bryce Hammond in *Phantoms*

If *Whispers* begins like a psychological thriller with overtones of a slasher film, *Phantoms* opens like a tautly directed '50s monster movie. Home to the mountain ski resort of Snowfield comes Dr. Jennifer Paige and her kid sister Lisa. It is late afternoon in early September, the off-season, and the alpine hamlet is quiet. Too quiet. A predatory stillness lies upon Snowfield. It is the silence of mass death: the town is now a necropolis.

At her home, Jennifer discovers the first body: her maid Hilda. The condition of the corpse—bloated, decomposition unnaturally arrested, every inch severely bruised—is inexplicable. And its face is locked in the rictus of a scream. Sudden death has struck the people of Snowfield. Hundreds are dead. As twilight blankets the decimated town, Jennifer and Lisa begin one of their many explorations of Snowfield, explorations that will lead them to a confrontation with a monster immeasurably old and incalculably evil, yet horrifyingly familiar.

Unlike *Whispers* and *Darkfall*, *Phantoms* is set in a pastoral locale: an isolated resort nestled in the Sierras. Snowfield is a serene, upscale community, a haven from "the rude world where violence and unkindness were disconcertingly common" (39)—from the world of *Whispers*. But in even so secure a setting, horror can erupt from the very fabric of the environment. For in *Phantoms*, as in so many modern horror novels, "there's no safety anywhere" (141).

Phantoms is the monster tale as police procedural. It is built around a series of investigations aimed at solving "the mystery of Snowfield" (56): who (or what) killed the town? Jenny and Lisa—later joined by Sheriff Bryce Hammond and several deputies from nearby Santa Mira, and, later still, by an Army research team—ceaselessly explore the decimated town, seeking survivors and answers. They are men and women of reason: systematic, scientific, rational. And much of *Phantoms* examines the responses of such people to the presence of an unknown Evil, which has visited Snowfield in the form of the monster of the piece: the Ancient Enemy.

Like Hilary, Tony, and Joshua in *Whispers*, the investigators in *Phantoms* consider a series of more-or-less plausible explanations for the death of the town: plague, radiation, poison, toxic waste, a mutant strain of rabies, even—later, when when the siege of Snowfield has begun anew and more radical alternatives seem in order—invasion from outer space. None comes close to the truth.

For the truth is inaccessible by reason alone. In *Whispers*, truth could be uncovered beneath layers of unreliable public myth; in *Phantoms* more primal means are required. Jennifer Paige learns this early in the novel. She is in the home of friends, Tom and Karen Oxley. Tom and Karen have been slaughtered; their corpses are in the den. And Jennifer wants very badly to call for help, but she knows the phones to be dead. Then the Oxleys' phone rings. Answering it, Jennifer hears only silence, but she senses on the line a presence "unspeakably malevolent; perfectly, purely evil" (57):

> She was well educated, a woman of reason and logic, not even mildly superstitious. Thus far, she had attempted to solve the mystery of Snowfield by applying the tools of logic and reason. But for the first time in her life, they had utterly failed her. Now deep in her mind, something...*shifted,* as if an enormously heavy iron cover were being slid off a dark pit in her subconscious.... Virtually on the level of racial memory stored in the genes, she sensed what was happening in Snowfield. The knowledge was within her; however, it was so alien, so fundamentally illogical, that she resisted it, fighting hard to suppress the superstitious terror that boiled up within her. (56)

And, later in the novel, when Sheriff Hammond converses with the creature (via a computer terminal), he feels the same awareness, a "primitive superstitious terror," and senses that he is "in the presence of something evil, ancient, and...familiar" (301). Like Jenny, Bryce understands intuitively that reason alone cannot comprehend, let alone combat, the evil that has come to Snowfield. Consciously, the answers he seeks elude him, but:

> ...perhaps he did know. Deep down. Instinctively.
> If only he could reach inside himself, down past his
> civilized veneer which embodied so much skepticism,
> if he could reach into his racial memory, he might
> find the truth about the thing that had seized and
> slaughtered the people of Snowfield. (302)

Linked to this failure of reason and logic as deductive tools is the impotence of technology and its appropriation by Evil. Once Sheriff Hammond has gotten a look at the graveyard that was Snowfield, he calls in an investigative research team, a well-equipped group of scientists and support troops from the Army Medical Corps led by General Galen Copperfield. These are the experts, the scientists. Remote and forbidding in their decontamination suits, wandering in and out of their mobile field laboratories, they are the ultimate symbols of rationality. To Jennifer they're "the cavalry" come to the rescue: "The specialists had arrived. Like most Americans, she had enormous faith in specialists, in technology, and in science. Soon they would understand what had killed Hilda and...all the others" (206).

But they don't. Copperfield's technocrats are initially no more *successful* at solving the mystery of Snowfield than were Jenny and Bryce. Their investigations and analyses uncover many facts, but no answers. And their leader's intellectual rigidity leads only to terror and death. Ignoring Bryce's protestations, Copperfield insists on considering only possibilities that he and his team have been trained to handle: nerve gas, virus, poison, and the like. This attitude has infected his team of scientists, who "appeared determined to *force* the evidence to conform to their preconceived notions of what they would find in Snowfield" (221). This narrowness of vision leads Copperfield to send one of his support troops into a walk-in meat locker and thus into the tender embrace of the monster.

Ultimately, however, the depredations of the monster force the surviving members of Copperfield's team to a new open-mindedness, and they are then able to use their scientific knowledge and man-made technology to defeat Evil. It is, in fact, one of Copperfield's scientists—a geneticist named Sara Yamaguchi—who discovers the Ancient Enemy's weakness: since it is a creature of living, carbon-based tissue, its "delicate chemical balance" (364) can be destabilized by, of all things, a man-made, genetically-engineered microorganism. That it is technology and not religion or magic that ultimately overcomes the threat, restoring an uncertain order, is consistent with the science-fictional underpinnings of *Phantoms*.

Technology, the symbol of reason in the modern world, is impotent unless informed by instinct. And it is controlled by the Beast. The Ancient Enemy uses the telephone to terrorize its prey, manipulates the public power supply of Snowfield, communicates with its intended victims via computer terminal, and seizes control of the suit-to-suit radios of Copperfield's crisis team. Over phone lines and radios, the beast sings of nature, of animals and humans in torment. And sometimes, it sings with the voice of a child:

> Although it was a child's voice, tender and fragile, it nevertheless contained...something that shouldn't be in a child's voice. A profound lack of innocence. Knowledge, perhaps. Yes. Too much knowledge of too many terrible things. Menace. Hatred. Scorn. It wasn't audible on the surface of the lilting song, but it was there beneath the surface, pulsing and dark and immeasurably disturbing. (283)

This theme—that technology, being morally neutral, can be made the handmaiden of evil—recurs in many of Koontz's novels, notably in *Darkfall*.

By combining instinct and reason, the humans in Snowfield deduce part of the truth of the Ancient Enemy: the (decidedly non-human) monsters that seem to control the town are manifestations of but a single entity, a mimic, a shape-changer. Catching on fast, Jenny explains that it "can impersonate anyone or any animal that it's previously fed on" (329), and "can assume the shape of anything it has absorbed *and* anything it can imagine" (331). Able to control its own DNA, the monster manifests itself in a variety of guises, many of which are images drawn from the grade-B SF/horror films of the '50s: "an obscenely fat black spider the size of a pony" (398), "an enormous hound" (399) with sulphurous breath, a "crab the size of a car" (332), a winged serpent, even the devil himself.

But the full story is told by an outsider, Dr. Timothy Flyte. Like Rita Yancy in *Whispers* (and many other figures in Koontz's novels), Flyte is the Outsider Who Knows. He knows precisely what is going on in Snowfield, for he has made the Ancient Enemy the focus of his life's work. By training an archeologist, by nature a visionary, Flyte had been ostracized by the academic community for writing a book in which he attributes the hundreds of unexplained mass disappearances that punctuate recorded history to "pre-historic creature[s]" (241) like the one now feeding on Snowfield. Koontz depicts Flyte as an amiable eccentric, "a character right out of Dickens" (155), but leaves no doubt that he is eminently qualified to answer questions that, for Jenny and Bryce, are of more than academic interest.

The Ancient Enemy is as appropriate a symbol of Evil as one could want. It is a creature of paradox: shapeless, it nonetheless embraces all shapes. A denizen of the underworld of storm drains and tunnels, caverns and watercourses, the monster, like the subconscious evil in the humans on which it feeds, moves beneath the surface and appears without warning in unpredictable forms. And, like evil, this protean creature is "by nature unspecific" (304). Underground, it assumes its natural state: amorphous, undifferentiated protoplasm. But above ground, it can be anything: a dog, a human, a demon from the Christian or Lovecraftian mythos—even the Devil.

Koontz describes this creature from "the bowels of the earth" (402) using metaphors of filth and slime. His account of its first appearance in its natural state, erupting from an open manhole on a street in Snowfield, is a blend of the excretory and the phallic. Rendered as always in Koontz's sledgehammer prose, it is positively orgasmic:

> Abruptly, something rose out of that hole, came from the storm drain below the street, rose and rose into the twilight, shuddering, smashing up into the air with tremendous power, a dark and pulsating mass, like a flood of sewage, except that it was not a fluid but a jellied substance that formed itself into a column almost as wide as the hole from which it continued to extrude itself in an obscene, rhythmic gush. It grew and grew: four feet high, six feet, eight... (323)

Oozing blistering digestive juices, this omnivorous, thoroughly malevolent "ameboid thing" of pseudopods and tentacles explodes out of the grounds and buildings of Snowfield like a Lovecraftian vision of cosmic evil. (At one point Koontz nods to Lovecraft, referring to the survivors as "in the middle of a Lovecraftian nightmare" (281).) Late in the novel we learn that until it rose into the caverns beneath Snowtop Mountain to feed, the creature dwelled in the icy darkness of deep ocean trenches, hibernating, Cthulhu-like, in a "dreamlike state" (408). Yet, the allusion to Lovecraft seems not entirely apt: as we soon learn, the nature of Evil in *Phantoms*, embodied in and symbolized by the Ancient Enemy, is quite different from that in the Lovecraftian cosmos. So why evoke Lovecraftian horror?

Misdirection: in structure, imagery, and atmosphere, *Phantoms* is filled with red herrings. These feints lead us to expect a particular kind of Evil, one familiar from the genre, to be at the heart of the novel—when in fact Koontz has something very different in mind. From its spooky beginning, in which all the inhabitants of an isolated town are discovered to have vanished (remember the opening of the 1957 film *The Beginning of the End?*), to its effects-filled finale, in which a band of survivors face a vast, amorphous monster (*The Blob*), *Phantoms* plays like a '50s monster movie. Its inexplicable horrific deaths, ominous silences, unseen presences, and preposterous monsters (a gigantic moth, a spider-thing, tentacles galore) evoke the stark, vivid images of the black-and-white, grade B horror film. This referential quality is reinforced by Koontz's style—he is one of the most cinematic of contemporary horror novelists—which encompasses the literary equivalents of everything from jump cuts to zooms.

Koontz doesn't miss a trick. The novel's effectively spooky atmospherics, which often soar to Lovecraftian heights of horror, its ramblings about ancient evil, and its many invocations of Christian symbols of evil, all seduce us genre-conscious readers into anticipating a familiar resolution: that the Ancient Enemy is either religious (the Devil), supernatural (a Lovecraftian monster), or preternatural (*e.g.*, a giant crab). Just as Bruno Frye seems, for a time, to be back from the dead, the very model of a modern genre zombie, the monsters of Snowfield appear to be horrors, perhaps supernatural, perhaps not, unrelated to man—except insofar as they want to kill him.

Throughout the novel, Koontz adroitly manipulates the elements of Christian theology. During the siege of Snowfield, the Ancient Enemy mocks human faith, exploiting belief in the religious supernatural to demoralize or enslave its prey. Christian images abound. And explicit references to Christianity come thick and fast during the creature's dialogue-by-computer with Bryce Hammond. It has seized control of one of General Copperfield's terminals and is speaking, via flickering images on the screen, in tones that ridicule the tenets of human faith: "JESUS IS DEAD. GOD IS DEAD...I AM ALIVE." Asked its name, the creature's answer recalls a host of demons from Christian theology: "I AM HABORYM. I AM A MAN WITH THREE HEADS—ONE HUMAN, ONE CAT, ONE SERPENT...I AM RANTAN...I AM PALLAMTRE...I AM AMLUTHIAS, ALFINA, EPYN, FUARD, BELIAL, OMGORMA, NEBIROS, BAAL, ELIGOR, AND MANY OTHERS...I AM ALL AND NONE. I AM NOTHING. I AM EVERYTHING" (308). And later in the novel the monster assumes the form of the most potent icon of Christian evil in the mythos: Lucifer himself.

But it's all a setup. The Ancient Enemy is neither Christian devil nor Lovecraftian monster; it is a creature of the prehistoric world. Originally amorphous and (presumably) morally neutral, it learned Evil from the only truly evil creature in the cosmos of the novel. Timothy Flyte explains:

> It's real, a creature of flesh—although not flesh like ours. It's not a spirit or a devil. Yet...in a way...I believe it is Satan. Because, you see, I believe it was this creature—or another like it, another monstrous survivor from the Mesozoic Era—that inspired the myth of Satan. In prehistoric times, men must have encountered one of these things, and some of them must have lived to tell about it. They naturally described their experiences in the terminology of myth and superstition. I suspect most of the demonic

> figures in the world's various religions are actually re-
> ports of these shape-changers, reports passed down
> through countless generations before they were at last
> committed to hieroglyphics, scrolls, and then print.
> They were reports of a very rare, very real, very dan-
> gerous beast...but described in the language of reli-
> gious myth. (345)

Thus does the religious sub-text of *Phantoms* subvert traditional genre notions of supernatural Evil.   According to its premise,
Evil originates not in Christian demonology nor in an uncaring Lovecraftian cosmos.   The source is man.   From "the knowledge and memories of those on whom it feeds" (345), from minds devoid of empathy,
compassion, or love, did the Ancient Enemy derive its cruel humor, its
penchant for sadism and mockery, and its viciousness.   Thus the Beast
is but a template on which has been impressed the unmediated evil of
man.

The "devil on a glass slide" in *Phantoms* also inverts the
Christian notion of evil: that human wickedness is but a reflection of
the existence of the Devil.   Jenny articulates Koontz's theme:

> ...maybe the only real devils are human beings, not
> all of us; not the species as a whole; just the ones
> who're twisted, the ones who somehow never acquire
> empathy or compassion.   If the shape-changer was the
> Satan of mythology, perhaps the evil in human beings
> isn't a reflection of the Devil; perhaps the Devil is
> only a reflection of the savagery and brutality of our
> own kind.   Maybe what we've done is...create the
> Devil in our own image.   (413)

Yet another explosion of religious references occurs when,
near the end of the novel, the dying monster beats a "Mephisthophelean
retreat," returning to its underworld of dark caverns and dank tunnels.
Eaten from within by man's genetically engineered microorganism, the
Ancient Enemy dies a fitting death: a death by plague, a death of le-
sions, suppurating sores, and massive tissue decomposition—a cancer-
ous death.   Koontz narrates its fate in terms expressly mythic and religious:

> It crept deeper, deeper, across the underworld
> river that flowed in Stygian darkness, deeper still,
> farther down into the infernal regions of the earth,
> into the chambers of Orcus, Hades, Osiris, Erebus,
> Minos, Loki, Satan....   It went deeper, down into Ja-
> hanna, into Gehenna, into Sheol, Abbadon, into the

Pit. Over the centuries it had eagerly assumed the
role of Satan and other evil figures, which men had
attributed to it, had amused itself by catering to their
superstitions. Now, it was condemned to a fate consistent with the mythology it had helped create...It
had been cast down. It had been damned. It would
dwell in darkness and despair for the rest of its life.
(409)

As if to show the sort of human that nourished his monster,
Koontz includes in *Phantoms* two examples of the worst of the species:
Fletcher Kale and Gene Terr. Kale is a real-estate agent—not, in itself,
reprehensible. But he is also the slayer of his wife and child. Early in
the novel, Sheriff Hammond breaks Kale's cover—like Bruno Frye, the
monster in Kale lurks beneath a seemingly normal surface. But Kale,
who possesses "animal cunning and suddenness" (63), easily escapes
and leaves Santa Mira, heading for Snowtop Mountain. Reveling in destruction and corruption, this wholly amoral sociopath is fitting fodder
for the Ancient Enemy.

Gene Terr (Jeeter) is no prize either. The leader of a motorcy-
cle gang called Demon Chrome, Jeeter spends his days and nights rap-
ing, murdering, and terrorizing innocents. Birds of a feather, he and
Kale immediately sense their dark kinship when they meet in the lime-
stone cave beneath Snowtop Mountain. There, erupting before their
jaded eyes, is the Ancient Enemy. Kale immediately becomes a believer: "...this was an apparition, a Hell-born presence that had
swarmed up from the Pit—just smell the sulphur, the scent of Satan!—and therefore *anything was* possible" (392). Kale thinks it a mere
demon, but Jeeter knows: "[I]t is from Hell, man. But it's no demon.
It's *Him. Him.* Lucifer." Cooperatively, the creature assumes the
form of a towering horned, winged visage—which his apostles greet
with "evangelical passion" (406).

The creature has learned well from man. Vindictive to the
last, it seduces Kale and Jeeter with promises of everlasting life (in
Hell) to agree to kill Bryce and Jenny. But this time, Evil fails. The
dying creature's plan is thwarted. Jeeter is shot. And Kale finds his
destiny: he too is felled by a microorganism. Bitten by a tick, Kale
contracts Rocky Mountain Spotted Fever and dies. It is no great loss.

The human monsters Fletcher Kale and Gene Terr are less
subtle representatives of Evil than Bruno Frye. And, unlike *Whispers*,
Phantoms posits that evil is a real and potent force that originates in
man. But like its predecessor, this novel critiques traditional images of
the monster from genre fiction, suggesting that B-movie monsters,
Lovecraftian horrors, and Christian demons are inadequate representatives of evil for the modern world. They remain useful only as
symbols or repositories of the evil that is the ultimate monster, man. In

his next novel, *Darkfall*, the theme of religious evil reappears, in a radically different way, and shares center stage with a quite different monster.

3.

THE RATS IN THE WALLS:
THE DEMON HORDE OF BABA LAVELLE

Tonight there are two kinds of darkness in this city, Lieutenant. First, there's that darkness which is merely the absence of light. And then there's that darkness which is the physical presence—the very manifestation—of the ultimate Satanic evil. That second and malignant form of darkness feeds upon and cloaks itself in the first and more ordinary kind of darkness, cleverly disguises itself. But it's out there!
—Carver Hampton in *Darkfall*

In its opening chapters, *Darkfall* seems to be a variation on *Whispers* and *Phantoms*, another monster-tale-as-police-procedural. Dimly-seen creatures—small, rat-like, with featureless, glowing eyes—stalk eleven-year-old Penny Dawson as her father Jack, a New York City homicide detective, and his partner Rebecca Chandler investigate a quartet of bizarre, drug-related murders. Some of the slayings occurred in locked rooms, and the victims were horribly mutilated: gazing at a corpse, Rebecca observes, "He looks...*chewed*" (28).

But *Darkfall* differs from its predecessors in both structure and theme. In this, the third panel in Dean Koontz's triptych of terror, religious Evil comes into its own. And the villain of the piece, the charming Baba Lavelle, with his psychically-directed pack of vicious, verminous, predatory demons, is one of Koontz's most compelling.

Lavelle is a Haitian *Bocor*—a voodoo priest who uses black magic. Tall, dark, handsome, and immutably evil, he is aptly characterized (by a prostitute) as "one smart, creepy, badass dude" (66). While investigating the murder of a drug dealer named Vince Vastagliano, Jack and Rebecca learn that Lavelle is trying to take over the New York City drug trade by using voodoo curses to kill off members of the ruling Carramazzas, a Mafia family who quite handily represent human evil in the novel. But these are merely rumors, and Rebecca isn't having any of it. She stridently insists that "[the killer] is just another psycho like all the psychos who're crawling out of the walls these days. There's nothing special or strange about him" (48).

But more inexplicable murders and a surprise visit with Don Gennaro Carramazza, the reptilian patriarch of the family ["The old man looked...like a snake in a thousand dollar suit." (130)] convince Rebecca that Lavelle is real. But on the subject of voodoo, she's adamant: "So he exists? That doesn't mean voodoo works!" (135). Before long a close encounter with Lavelle's little horde of horrors removes these last lingering doubts.

Iconographically, Lavelle functions in *Darkfall* as the shaman; symbolically, he is the embodiment of supernatural, religious evil— which in the universe of this novel exists as an independent force. Although Lavelle has struck an alliance with supernatural powers, his demeanor belies his nature: "his long association with evil had not given him a bleak, mournful or even sour aspect; he was a happy man...[who] virtually radiated self confidence" (110-111). With his noble face, elegant voice, and engaging laugh, Lavelle seems the very antithesis of villainy. But behind the charming smile, Evil lurks. Carver Hampton, a voodoo priest of white magic who counterbalances Lavelle in the novel, explains to Jack Dawson what he is up against:

> "He's an extremely powerful *Bocor*, Lieutenant. Not an amateur. Not your average spellcaster; he has the power of darkness, the ultimate darkness of death, the darkness of Hell, the darkness of the Other Side... he is very probably mad, insane;... That is a most formidable combination: evil beyond measure, madness, and the power of a masterfully skilled *Bocor*."
> (143-44)

Unlike Bruno Frye, the human monster of *Whispers*, Lavelle is no victim. He is simply evil. And, unlike the madness that infects Frye, Lavelle's insanity neither excuses nor explains his wickedness. It is psychopathy after the fact, icing on the cake of evil.

Baba Lavelle is right at home in New York City, which Koontz depicts as a cesspool of depravity where currents of evil course through slate-gray skies above blood-drenched streets:

> ...in this great city he had discovered an enormous reservoir of the power on which he depended in order to do his work: the infinitely useful power of evil... here, where so many people were crammed into such a relatively small piece of land, here where a score or two of murders were committed every week, here where assaults and rapes and robberies and burglaries numbered in the tens of thousands—even hundreds of thousands—every year, here where there were an army of hustlers looking for an advantage, legions of con men searching for marks, psychos of every twisted sort, perverts, punks, wife-beaters, and thugs

almost beyond counting—this was where the air was
flooded with raw currents of evil that you could see
and smell and feel. (109-10)

Lavelle draws strength and succor from "vast, tenebrous rivers
of evil energy" that surge above and through Manhattan. Koontz treats
this metaphor almost literally: these psychic streams are "Ethereal
rivers, yes. Of no substance. Yet the energy of which they were composed was real, lethal, the very stuff with which Lavelle could achieve
virtually any result he wished" (110). This depiction of Evil contrasts
strikingly with that in *Whispers* or *Phantoms*: here Evil is real, "a
cosmic power, beyond human comprehension" (145). As *Darkfall* progresses, Koontz will adhere to this explicitly religious notion, introducing Good as an (equally cosmic) counterpoint to Evil, and constructing a narrative that hurtles arrow-straight towards a classic confrontation between the two.

The imagistic pattern of the novel evolves from the classic
identification of Evil with darkness, Good with light. Not surprisingly,
Lavelle is a creature of darkness, "at home in shadows," for "darkness,
after all, was a part of him" (198). (The good shaman Carver Hampton
is also a black man, but he is associated with light. When, late in the
novel, an increasingly desperate Jack Dawson goes to Hampton's
Harlem voodoo shop to plead for help, he finds every light in the place
blazing.) Darkness not only cloaks the elusive Lavelle, it succors him,
heals him, caresses, and embraces him: "He suckled on it. Nothing
else soothed as completely and as deeply as the darkness" (276).

Lavelle is motivated by the simplest of reasons: he's out to
avenge his brother Gregory, who was murdered by the Carramazza
family. Actually, it is not so much the rending of filial bonds that has
incensed Lavelle as the slight to his ego: "The murder of my brother is
an insult to me," he rages at Jack. "It diminishes me. It mocks me. I
cannot tolerate that.... Blood must flow. The floodgates of death must
be opened. Oceans of pain must sweep them away, all who mocked me
by touching my brother" (155).

Lavelle's vendetta is a family affair: he directs his supernatural agents to slaughter the wife, daughter, grandchildren, and brother of
Don Gennaro Carramazza. Indeed, the motive force of *Darkfall* and
one of the novel's central thematic preoccupations is threat of fragmentation of the family. Every major character has suffered a loss that has
fractured his family. Jack's wife Linda—Penny and Davey's mother—
was killed in an automobile accident. While Rebecca was a child her
father, then her mother were both blown away by a junkie—which horror was followed by the lingering death by cancer of her grandfather.
(Out of Rebecca's loss grew her unyielding hostility and inability to
trust or love. She and Jack are well-matched adversaries; she's as cal-
lous and cold as he is sensitive and caring. They squabble constantly.)

The threat of fragmentation of the family also dominates the second half of the novel, in which police procedural gives way to chase thriller. Once Jack and Rebecca cease bickering and fall in love, the formation of a new family—Jack, Rebecca, and Penny and Davey—seems in the offing. But Lavelle is on to Jack, and to scare him off uses the rituals of voodoo magic to direct the daemonic horde to kill his kids. (Lavelle's least endearing trait is the delight he takes in the slaughter of children. He can hardly wait to send his capering demons out after Penny and Davey, and displays a zest that is downright unseemly: "He didn't mind killing children. He looked forward to it. There was a special exhilaration in the murder of the very young. He licked his lips" [163].)

From this point on, one chase follows another. Jack and Rebecca fight their way through a violent snowstorm to save Jack's kids, whom he has ensconced in the apartment of his dippy sister-in-law, Faye Jamison. Then, pursued by Lavelle's implacable, ravening devils, the incipient family escapes into the blizzard-lashed streets of New York. Finally, they split up. Rebecca and the kids seek refuge in St. Patrick's cathedral while Jack sets off for Lavelle's lair.

Although the battle for the family in *Darkfall* takes place in one of the most populous cities in the world, it is fought in isolation. During the first half of the novel, the first snowstorm of the season becomes a blizzard of epic proportions. Hammering the streets of Manhattan, the tempest isolates the beleaguered family. Snow transforms the cityscape, obscuring and hiding its familiar features, and creating an undifferentiated landscape of white violence against which the innocent are pursued.

To carry out his schemes, Lavelle infests New York with a plague of vicious, predatory monsters. To describe these creatures, which vivify the omnipresence of Evil, Koontz uses an extravagant range of tropes from nature, particularly those of reptiles and vermin. In many respects, the horde is like the Ancient Enemy in *Phantoms*. Lavelle's demons are denizens of the underworld, of darkness: they creep through the walls of apartment buildings and ventilation systems of hotels, slither through subway tunnels and storm drains beneath city streets, and lurk in the shadowed corners of parking garages. They may erupt anywhere, without warning, to terrorize and butcher innocent and guilty alike. Like the shape-changer, the horde is comprised of many forms. And they arouse an intense instinctual response in their prey. Their first victim (in the novel), a drug dealer with "the imagination of a tree stump" (12), senses what he cannot see: "[H]is subconscious knew what it was, and that was why he fled from it in a blind panic, as wide-eyed and spooked as a dumb animal reacting to a bolt of lightning" (13).

For much of the novel, Koontz keeps the creatures off stage. Their victims see only a "vague impression of...something small, about the size of a large rat; sleek and streamlined and slithery like a rat" (56). But though shadows enshroud the shape of the fiend, nothing can hide its merciless, glowing eyes. Aglow with hell-fire, these eyes are windows to barren souls:

> They appeared not to be eyes at all; they had no pupils or irises, no solid tissue that he could discern. They were just empty sockets in the creature's mal-formed skull, crude holes from which radiated a harsh, cold, brilliant light...the very worst aspect of those mad eyes [was] the death-cold, hate-hot, soul-withering feeling they imparted when you dared to meet them. Looking into the thing's eyes, Jack felt both physically and spiritually ill. (251-52)

When Koontz finally describes the capering horde, in one of the most baroque renderings of Evil in modern horror fiction, he pulls out all the stops:

> Beyond the worm-thing, the security foyer was crawling with other, different devils, all of them small, but all of them so incredibly vicious and grotesque in appearance that Jack began to shake and felt his bowels turn to jelly. There were lizard-things in various sizes and shapes. Spider-things. Rat-things. Two of the man-form beasts, one of them with a tail, the other with a sort of cock's comb on its head and along its back. Dog-things. Crablike, fe-line, snakelike, beetle-form, scorpionlike, dragonish, clawed and fanged, spiked and spurred and sharply horned *things*. Perhaps twenty of them. No. More than twenty. At least thirty. They slithered and skit-tered across the mosaic-tile floor, and they crept tena-ciously up the walls, their foul tongues darting and fluttering ceaselessly, teeth gnashing and grinding, *eyes* shining. (282)

This is Evil diverse and varied, secretive and intelligent, implacable and twisted, omnipresent and, just maybe, unstoppable.

The depredations of the demon horde focus the first half of *Darkfall*, where, as in the first half of *Phantoms* and the latter part of *Whispers*, Koontz's heroes ceaselessly investigate and speculate, trying to solve the *mystery* of the Nature of the Beast. Ultimately, they learn from Carver Hampton that Lavelle's devils are spiritual beings risen from Hell that acquired their shapes from the earth.

Behind Lavelle and his "small assassins" (239) is the "great, malevolent pantheon" of the gods of voodoo, the gods of *Congo* and *Petro*. This legion of malefic deities lends a religious dimension to *Darkfall* that was absent from its predecessors. And this expressly religious context supports the apocalyptic threat that comes to dominate the novel. By cracking open the Gates of Hell to release his demon horde, Lavelle has inadvertently raised the stakes. For just on the other side of the entryway that he now controls are "vast multitudes of monstrous creatures [that] will come forth to slaughter the innocent, the meek, the good, and the just. Only the wicked will survive, but they'll find themselves living in Hell on Earth" (315). It is the ultimate threat: biblical Armageddon.

Koontz realizes the religious dimension of Evil through the motif of the voodoo ritual. Voodoo codifies many elements of religion-in-the-abstract: gods good and evil, rules and rituals, moral imperatives and the consequences of ignoring them. As Carver Hampton explains to Jack, it is "a synthesis of many doctrines that usually war against one another—everything from Christianity and Judaism to sun-worship and pantheism" (328). Voodoo thus functions in the novel as generic religion.

But the voodoo practiced by the priests of *Darkfall* is notable for what it omits: it is voodoo without zombies. The goals of most rituals of West Indian voodoo, as described in such (nonfiction) books as Hugh B. Cave's *Haiti: Highroad to Adventure* (1952), are the displacement of the soul followed by possession by a dark god, or the resuscitation of a corpse which is then enslaved. Such are the ends sought also by evil priests in genre novels by Cave and stories by Henry S. Whitehead, Robert Bloch, Carl Jacobi, and others. But Baba Lavelle uses rites and incantations not to possess his victims, but to command the demon horde to slaughter them. He also uses voodoo rituals to solicit advice from his dark benefactors—via his radio.

Lavelle is under siege. He has been unable to humiliate, threaten, or otherwise turn aside the relentless Jack Dawson, whom he knows to be "one of those rare individuals, that one in ten thousand, who could do battle with even the most masterful *Bocor* and be reasonably certain of victory" (198). Insecure and indecisive, he switches on a nearby radio and tunes in the gods. Muttered chants and incantations change the dead air of an unused frequency into "a voice of dust and mummified remains...a voice of infinite age, as bitterly cold as the night between the stars, jagged and whispery and evil.... If God had given snakes the power of speech, this was what they would have sounded like" (200-01). The god's advice—kill the Dawson kids *now*—is just what Lavelle wants to hear.

Lavelle's use of a radio to chat with the gods is but one instance of the appropriation of technology by evil in *Darkfall*—a motif that was present also in *Whispers* and *Phantoms*. In his rituals, Lavelle uses photographs of Penny and Davey, rather than the stereotypical voodoo dolls. And he uses the telephone to terrorize Carver and Jack. In one of the most effective scenes in the novel, he phones Jack, who at the time is wading through the snow outside Carver's shop in Harlem. Through hypnosis, Lavelle transports Jack to a place of dreams. The buildings and cars and streets around him "evaporate," replaced by a "creeping mist, a white-white mist that was like a movie theater screen splashed with brilliant light but with no image" (147). In this scene, which prefigures the pursuit later in the novel of Jack, Rebecca, Penny, and Davey through the snow-clogged streets of Manhattan, the stark dialectic of *Darkfall* is clear: the universe is reduced to good (Jack) and evil (Lavelle on the phone).

In this simple dialectic, unmitigated Evil is opposed by unalloyed Good, embodied in the characters of Carver Hampton and Jack Dawson. Like Evil, Good is a palpable (though ethereal) force with its own pantheon of gods, the *Rada* of voodoo myth. And Carver Hampton, the *Houngon* of white magic, is their priest. Through most of the novel, Hampton seems to serve the same function as did Rita Yancy in *Whispers* and Timothy Flyte in *Phantoms*: the authentic source of wisdom and truth. Thus, he instructs Jack about the threat Lavelle represents and the "special power" (198) Jack can command in his war with evil. But unlike Yancy and Flyte, Hampton is an active force for good. He leads Jack through the ritual of purification Jack must undergo, and, in spite of his understandable reluctance to do battle with Lavelle, accompanies Jack to the *Bocor*'s hideout.

Jack's "special power" is the most problematical aspect of the novel. Because he is "a man whose soul bears the stains of only the most minor sins," Jack is immune to supernatural Evil. In his brightly-lit Harlem shop, Carver Hampton tries to explain to an understandably skeptical Dawson:

> A *Bocor* has no power whatsoever to harm a righteous man. The righteous are well-armored.... By the manner in which you've led your life, you've earned immunity to the dark powers, immunity to the curses and charms and spells of sorcerers like Lavelle. You cannot be touched. (322)

This moralistic, explicitly religious premise that underlies Koontz's mainstream horror thriller almost turns it into an ecclesiastical polemic.

In his war with evil, the righteous man possesses two tools: the rituals of magic and instincts. *Darkfall* is riddled with rituals; they are vital to the schemes of Baba Lavelle, who must adhere to the rites of his gods in order to control the Hell-born spawn he summons. But the rituals of man, the rites of reason, are portrayed as ineffectual. Indeed, *Darkfall*, like *Phantoms*, questions the efficacy of rationalism in the face of true Evil. The exponent of rationalism in the novel is Jack's partner, Rebecca Chandler. Like Galen Copperfield in *Phantoms*, Rebecca insists on sticking to procedure; she is perpetually arguing that Jack's effectiveness is mitigated by "an excessive degree of open-mindedness" (49), especially insofar as the supernatural is concerned, and insisting that he follow standard investigative methods. But just as it is the racial memory prodding at Jennifer Paige and Bryce Hammond in Snowfield that clues them in to the nature of the Ancient Enemy, it is Jack's "hunches" that lead him to the truth. And to vanquish Lavelle, Jack must violate and then dispense with the rituals of police procedures.

In *Darkfall*, as in *Whispers* and *Phantoms*, rigid adherence to reason, logic, and rational procedures isn't merely unsuccessful; it's downright dangerous. (Nor is such a practice rational, a point made by the quotation from Francis Bacon with which Koontz opens the last part of *Darkfall*: "There is superstition in avoiding superstition.") Reason remains a potent tool, but rationalism uninformed by instinct, flexibility of mind, and compassion is but an empty artifice, serving those who follow it only as a means of avoiding fear—until Evil shoves it down their throats. This critique of pure reason is a thematic cornerstone of Koontz's novels.

Still, the cosmos according to *Darkfall* is a far cry from that of *Whispers*, where the concept of evil all but vanishes in the complex of psychoses of the Frye family history, or that of *Phantoms*, where the source of evil is man's mind. These novels do not permit the unambiguous (and reassuring) moral alignment of *Darkfall*. Yet, in all three novels Good and Evil transcend human comprehension. Man is not irrelevant to the conflict between cosmic good and evil, as in the more pessimistic streams of contemporary horror. Evil simply exists, and only through faith, love, duty, and courage can man hope to defeat it.

X.

DEAN KOONTZ'S *TWILIGHT EYES*:

ART AND ARTIFACT

BY MICHAEL R. COLLINGS

In 1973 Dean Koontz published what has been called his first "major novel," *Hanging On*, followed the next year by the mainstream *After the Last Race*, a hardcover publication from Atheneum. To say that his career began at that point would be foolhardy, of course; between 1968 and 1973, he had published fifteen science-fiction novels through Lancer, Ace, Bantam, and others; and several volumes of short fiction and non-fiction.[1]

In a sense, however, *Hanging On* did represent a shift in Koontz's career—one intensified over the years as he moved away from narrowly defined science fiction into contemporary psychological horror with such works as *Night Chills* (1976). *Nightmare Journey* (1975) represented a swan song to strict science fiction, while his acquisition of a word processor allowed for a depth of complexity and thoroughgoing revision in recent novels such as *Strangers* that is not found in his earlier genre pieces. As a result, one characteristic of his present style is an intense awareness of character and voice, developed through multiple rewritings. For this reason, he insists that over the decade between 1975-85 his writing changed tremendously (Letter, 14 Jan. 86).

What he has accomplished since, including such ambitious works as *Phantoms*, *Whispers*, *Strangers*, and the "Leigh Nichols" novels, defines a clearly different approach to the art of fiction from such slimmer, less complex volumes as *Anti-Man* (1970), *A Werewolf Among Us* (1973), the pseudonymous *Invasion* (1975, as Aaron Wolfe) or even *Nightmare Journey*, with its SF variations on Odyssean wanderings.

With the publication of *Twilight Eyes* (1985) from Christopher Zavisa's Land of Enchantment press, Koontz demonstrated yet another permutation in a career noted for constant exploration. Joining the ranks of such notables as Robert A. Heinlein, Arthur C. Clarke, Stephen King, and Jack Vance, Koontz became involved in the publication of a limited edition, lavishly illustrated, specialty house novel.

Publishers such as Donald M. Grant, Scream/Press, and Dark Harvest have discovered the advantages of creating limited, collectible artifacts; but there is more to *Twilight Eyes* than merely an attempt to capitalize on a literary trend. Koontz's fiction consistently hovers at the edge of generic borders. Such novels as *Phantoms* and *Strangers*, for example, blend mainstream fiction with fantasy, psychological suspense with action-adventure, horror with science fiction. It may be a trademark of Koontz, in fact, that generic considerations become increasingly difficult as he develops, a point clearly made by *Twilight Eyes*—one part psychological case study, one part self-revelatory first-person narrative, one part horror, and one part science fiction.

Beyond this, however, *Twilight Eyes* represents an increasingly important trend in science fiction and fantasy publishing. Just as the novel draws upon several generic backgrounds and intertwines the strands into a unified whole, so the book itself depends for its impact—visual and verbal—upon a complex of interrelated forms. The *book* has become the focus of attention, almost in spite of the power of its text.

Others have noted this tendency, and decried what they see as abuses in the practice. In the November 1986 issue of *Fantasy Review*, Jack L. Chalker stimulated a spirited debate with his criticism of Stephen King's *The Eyes of the Dragon* (1984) as published by Philtrum Press. Although Chalker makes several errors in titles (he refers first to *The Eyes of the Overworld*, then to Pequod Press), the series of articles staunchly defends small-press specialty houses that have become experts in the publication of books-as-art. What many critics of such presses miss is that books on the order of *The Eyes of the Dragon* (Philtrum Press), *The Talisman* (Donald Grant), *Skeleton Crew* (Scream/Press), or *Twilight Eyes* (Land of Enchantment) try to do much more than merely convey a narrative. In the hands of a specialty press, the book becomes, as it were, a self-conscious artifact, with every element important to the final impact.

If in earlier publications illustrations were intended primarily to elucidate (or at least visualize) episodes or characters from a story, the art in contemporary limited editions aspires to much more. It becomes part of the narrative, an inherent structure that works *with* the verbal text in creating the narrative.

Even so, Koontz has suggested that many of the limited, illustrated editions are "not as special as they ought to be," an observation that led him, in company with Phil Parks and Chris Zavisa, to attempt to create "a truly *amazing* book" (Letter, 31 Jan. 86).

In the case of *Twilight Eyes*, they have succeeded; Parks's artwork and Zavisa's production design literally establish the reader's expectations before the author has had the chance to communicate a word.

Of course, to a marginal degree at least, such is always the case with a book. Cover art has a single primary purpose—to entice the reader into the text. In mass-market publishing, however, the cover art occasionally contradicts the intent of the novel itself, or at best illustrates a single (and often inherently unimportant but visually stimulating) episode. Nor is it unheard of that a novel embellished by the most blatant "bodice-ripping" cover art may have no such scene in it at all.

But with the illustrated limited edition, the function of artwork—both as illustration and for its own sake—expands enormously. The artist can work more deeply into the text, rather than having to be satisfied with imposing a single visual image upon it. Although several publishers of limited editions have removed artwork entirely (*i.e.*, limiteds of Robert A. Heinlein's *Job* or Arthur C. Clarke's *2001*, the Putnam limited of Frank Herbert's *God Emperor of Dune*, or the Donald I. Fine limited of Theodore Sturgeon's *Godbody*, none of which even use cover art), in other cases—spectacularly in the case of *Skeleton Crew* and *The Talisman*—the artwork becomes an inherent part of an art form composed of the author's words, the artists' visual renderings of those words, and the publisher's joining of the two.

The production of *Twilight Eyes* was just such a conscious interplay of efforts. Koontz has explained that the text was completed before the artwork, and that there was no direct influence on him from either artist or publisher in constructing the text; after that point, however, author, artist, and publisher worked closely:

> ...text was completed first, with no input from the artist. However, as Phil Parks and Chris Zavisa went through the manuscript, choosing scenes for illustrations, we were on the telephone with one another two and three times a week for months. They bounced their ideas off me, and I bounced some off them, and although I must say that the genius of the finished product is more their work than mine, it was nevertheless much more collaborative than the usual illustrated novel. (Letter, 31 Jan. 86)

The meshing of narrative and artwork is particularly effective in *Twilight Eyes*, in large part because of the close collaboration among principals. Koontz explains that the three of them agreed upon guidelines for the artwork:

1. The illustrations would intrigue rather than explain—that is, no individual artwork would reveal critical plot elements and thus reduce suspense for readers who thumbed through the text first. Instead, each illustration only becomes fully effective in the context of the words, as word and art build upon each other to a final impact more dramatic than either could create alone.

2. The artwork would not merely function as illustration, making visual the characters and setting of the novel. Instead, it would become an essential part of the imagistic patterning of *Twilight Eyes*; Parks's work would accentuate the sense of menace, the overriding tone of melancholy, and the vibrant colors of the carnival—which in turn would mask the underlying horrors, both in Koontz's words and in Parks's artwork.

3. The artwork would be precisely that—*artwork* rather than illustration. Instead of being isolated on separate pages (often pages of a different texture than the rest of the novel, further separating the verbal and the visual), only approximately related to the movement of the narrative, Parks's work would be literally integrated into Koontz's words.

4. The artwork would follow the novel's predominant light-dark imagery, not only in the surface representations, but also in theme.

At the smallest level, these concerns include the ribbon motifs used throughout to separate chapter parts. On a more complex level, they include carefully designed pages on which the illustrations establish and define—or contradict and disrupt—the boundaries of print. The last page of Chapter Nine, for example, contains only eight lines of text, extending from the top margin down two inches or so. Yet along the entire right hand side and extending into the binding, Parks incorporates a sketch of the edge of a carnival tent; a hand reaches upward to pull it back, as if the person were about to enter. It functions as an ideal visualization of the last line of text—"Trembling, I went inside"—and at the same time visually links the conclusion of one chapter with the beginning of the next. The reader is drawn forcibly across the page: from the last line of Koontz's chapter, to the darkest panels of Parks's carnival tent and downward, to the reaching fingers protruding just beyond the fabric into white space. From there the eye follows the line of wrist and forearm until it disappears into the binding—and the reader's eye is now level with the opening of Chapter Ten. The drawing has not only illustrated the text, but elucidated it and facilitated its reading as well, a technique used consistently throughout the novel.

  The importance of artwork to *Twilight Eyes* becomes apparent even before one opens the volume. *Twilight Eyes* boasts an unusually effective wrap-around dustjacket that itself meets the four criteria: it intrigues and invites the reader into the narrative as it evokes the carnival setting; yet at the same time it avoids a programmatic interpretation. The central figure clearly represents a carousel horse, but at the same time other touches imbue it with implicit threat: the increasingly dark background as the viewer's eyes move up the page; the wooden horse's wildly flaring eye surrounded by the nimbus-like mane; the taut arch of muscle, curving away from the horse's terrified eyes and down along its neck—focusing the viewer's attention on an Escher-like effect as a carved ornament on the saddle reaches out and digs furrows into the horse's wooden side. There is no blood—nothing that obvious. But the cover ideally introduces the tone, mood, atmosphere, and theme of *Twilight Eyes*, with its layerings of reality and illusion, with its monsters existing beneath the *façade* of the normal and the everyday.

In the book itself, the same emphasis continues. The trade edition is bound in black with a gold-line stylized representation of the carousel horse. Koontz notes that even the choice of colors required intense deliberation:

> We considered going with something bright, daz-
> zling, to echo the flamboyant colors of a carnival, but
> ultimately we chose instead to emphasize the darkness
> of the story with black binding, hinting at the dazzle
> of the carnival only in the gold embossing of the
> horse's head. (Letter, 31 Jan. 86).

The signed edition used a dark-red binding, creating a different (and perhaps less effective) tone, but nonetheless fitting the general feeling of the novel.

The front and back endpages reproduce one of the double-page drawings from the text (*cf.* p. 34-35). On a surface level, they represent a character walking along a deserted fairway, either late in the evening or early in the morning. The character's strength, suggested by his musculature as it reflects the faint light of the rising/setting moon/sun, juxtaposes with the sinuous lines of the tents, the silent octopus ride, and the curves of the other rides. Immediately one senses that something is desperately wrong here. The ambiguity of time was intentional, since it allows for an entry in the front endpapers, as Carl Stanfeuss, alias Slim MacKenzie, first arrives at the Sombra Brothers Carnival—the action outlined in Chapter One. The back endpapers, on the other hand, represent an exit, as he leaves one of the carnival's stopover towns. Koontz notes that this complex of visual arrivals and departures was designed to complement the text itself.

The next element is the full-color, double-page title page. It serves two functions; it must provide the reader with the requisite information, and it must bridge "the real world of the publisher-artist-writer-reader with the fantasy world of the story. "By putting the title page data *into* a scene from the novel, we tried literally to provide a point in the physical package where the book and the story interface and become one" (Koontz, Letter, 31 Jan. 86). The title page must be seen and studied to appreciate the full effect of its shadowy suggestions of violence and death. The outline in profile metaphorically parallels the monsters in the narrative; a knot in the wooden backdrop supporting tattered carnival posters provides an eye—almost painfully squinted— for the shadow. A tear in the upper left-hand poster corresponds to a ragged, animalistic ear, and the outline of the poster itself provides a hairline for the shadow. Similarly, four scratch-like lines in the wood suggest ribs, yet since they appear in the heart area, they also reflect the deep gouges in the carousel horse's flanks from the dustjacket. Again and again, details urge the reader to closer examination, to the multiple possibilities and ambiguities that lie at the heart of *Twilight Eyes*.

Finally, after atmosphere, mood, tone, theme, and subject have been explored by the artist and designer, we encounter the text itself. And at that stage, our appreciation of that text has been subtly but irrevocably altered by our responses to the artwork. The groundwork laid by Parks and Zavisa has given away little about the novel beyond setting and tone; yet, it has provided a more authentic entry *into* the world of the novel than most novels enjoy.

Koontz integrates much the same complexity into his text. As noted above, the novel blends psychological fiction, horror, fantasy, and science fiction (the latter perhaps the weakest in development and plausibility of the three).

Beyond that, however, *Twilight Eyes* attempts even more. Koontz said of his characters in general that each is carefully wrought:

> ...I strive (and the level of success varies) to create a character of depth and purity that, though not necessarily of a type immediately familiar to the reader from his daily life, swiftly becomes familiar in the early chapters; then the particular character's voice, if true, grows more transparent—and more real—page by page. This requires a horrible amount of rewriting. By the way of example, an average page is reworked anywhere from ten to twenty times, and the average number of reworkings of each page of *Whispers* was thirty-one.... If the technique I've just described is successful, the depth of the character and the true-to-life quality he possesses should not be immediately apparent, but should convince on a gut level straightaway and then, on later analysis, should be revealed as deeper than it seemed the first time through. (Letter, 14 Jan. 86)

In the passage, Koontz spoke of the range of his fiction; *Twilight Eyes*, he continues, was designedly opulent stylistically, with language functioning as a means of "swiftly and *totally*" immersing the reader into the narrative, in effect distracting the reader with language,

149

until suddenly the reader discovers "that the style has sucked him in like a whirlpool pulling down an exhausted swimmer."

Certainly one of the trademarks of *Twilight Eyes*, as of Koontz's work in general, is a meticulous awareness of language and linguistic effects. On the second page of the novel, he includes a passage describing Slim's first midnight view of the Sombra Brothers Carnival: "As I strolled through the lot, getting a feel for the place, I noticed how strangely white my own hands looked in that frosty luminescence, like the hands of a dead man, or those of a revenant returned to haunt the place of his demise" (9). Koontz handles the passage masterfully, using a possibly obscure word as *revenant*, then setting it into an environment that not only emphasizes it with the consonance of *returned* but actually defines the most important of its several meanings: "One who returns after death: a ghost." "Frosty luminescence" couples back to "strangely white," again providing connections in sound and sense to help interpret the passage. Such a sentence is typical of Koontz's care throughout *Twilight Eyes*.

Yet even such a structure pales next to the following sentence, the concluding sentence of the paragraph and a springboard into the action itself: "That was when I first perceived the lurking presence of Death among the rides and hanky-panks, and sensed, however dimly, that the carnival would be the site of murder and much blood" (9). In addition to the Lovecraftian echoes of "lurking presence" (again emphasized through alliteration with *perceived*), Koontz intensifies the effect of the description by casting it into metrical prose—almost into poetry. From "presence of Death" to the end, the sentence creates a virtually unbroken iambic meter, with the exception of two sequential unstressed syllables in "that the" and "and much." Even the oddly positioned modification of the last phrase—"of murder and much blood"—correlates to the inherent poetry of the line. And yet the devices are not overt or obvious. Instead, they function just under the reader's awareness, creating a line intensely powerful yet equally inexplicable.

Later on the same page, Koontz again hints at metric lines, this time almost rhyming "guilt," "spilled," and "killed," then catching the first word again in a metrical string: "Neither remorse nor guilt pursued me, for Uncle Denton had been one of them."

Again and again, Koontz writes lines that verge on poetry, that catch alliterative echoes from preceding sentences that rhyme across paragraphs and pages, that toss sound and sense back and forth like a carnival juggler—and in doing so repeat verbally the techniques of Parks and Zavisa employed visually.

All of this does not, of course, even approach a satisfying discussion of the novel itself. To do so would require at least a paper multiple times longer than this. Instead, it suggests that *Twilight Eyes* is in fact a rarity, even among limited, specialty-press editions. It is an artifact as well as a novel, a work of art that can be approached and apprehended on multiple levels: as book; as scaffold for illuminative art-work; as exploration of the potentials of language; as prose-poem of rich complexity; as cross-generic narrative that enlarges the traditional boundaries of horror, fantasy, and science fiction. Although a short work, it represents much of what Koontz has attempted in his longer, better-known (and thus more accessible) works,[2] and as such deserves close reading and re-reading.

XI.

FEMMES FATALES?

THE WOMEN PROTAGONISTS IN FOUR KOONTZ NOVELS

BY ELIZABETH MASSIE

Poor Rebecca. She and her police partner, Jack Dawson, are the targets of a hideous, supernatural power beset upon them by an evil voodoo priest. A good cop, yet personally defensive and cautious, Rebecca is drawn into the double peril of physical danger and emotional exposure when the evil threatens not only her partner and herself, but the lives of Jack's children as well.

Poor Mary. A bright and beautiful psychic, she finds that her ability to predict and prevent murders has become a terrible awareness that forewarns of her own impending, violent murder. She relies on her husband, Max, for strength, but as the danger presses closer, she finds she must face her forgotten yet horrible past in order to crush what would destroy her.

Poor Hilary. Intelligence and success as a screenwriter, and a solitary life, haven't protected her from the evils of the world. Her beauty has made her the target of a crazed and brutal sex-murderer. Quickness of mind protects her and allows her to kill her attacker, but she finds that his evil spirit may have, after all, allowed him to survive the grave to come after her again.

Poor Jenny and Rya. In an isolated Maine logging town, friends and neighbors are beginning to behave in strange and frightening ways. Jenny, a lovely young woman recovering from a failed marriage, must deal with her growing affection for Paul Annendale and with the increasing violence in her hometown. Rya, Paul's eleven-year-old daughter, mature and thoughtful, sees her brother beaten to death, and becomes the key to convincing her father that things are truly foul in the town of Black River.

In four of Dean Koontz's novels, *Darkfall*, *The Vision*, *Whispers*, and *Night Chills*, female characters play important if not the major roles within the tales. It is, of course, not often that one runs across a novel in which all the characters are of the same sex, especially not in the genre of horror fiction. Therefore, if a writer would make a character of the opposite sex realistic, particularly if that character is to be a major one, one whose feelings and motives are revealed to and understood by the reader, the writer has a basic challenge to face. When a writer creates a male and female-populated world, he or she must accept the task of making a world through which any reader, man or woman, would enjoy traveling for the time it takes to read the novel. A world in which, regardless of its evils and challenges and horrors, and even injustices, the reader can identify with the characters, or with *a character*, and thus come away feeling satisfied.

What gives a writer the ability to see across gender, or to create well-rounded, believable characters who are true to themselves? It might be easier to see what keeps a less competent writer from accomplishing this. There appear to be three main downfalls in creating a believable character of the opposite sex.

The first of these downfalls would be the writer's lack of insight. A writer unable to imagine a character's reactions in certain situations, unable to feel or sense the emotion and physical experiences of those characters, would certainly be unable to create living, breathing characters of the opposite sex. Of course, this writer would most likely have a difficult time with any character, and therefore be a less successful writer overall.

The second downfall would be lack of research. Not so much technical data or information, but personal information gained by taking the time to talk to and ask pertinent questions of the right people. A creative male writer could imagine to a certain degree what a female character might feel while giving birth. But perhaps it would better capture the essence if he could talk with women who have experienced this. Could he know, by imaging, that according to some women, both fear and expectation are dissolved until there is no past, no present, no future, no emotion, only pain? By relying solely on imagination, the writer invites the possibility of leaving out an important sensation such as a twinge, a pang, a detail.

The third downfall is prejudice, whether small or large, critical or complementary. A male writer who has a touch of chauvinism will undoubtedly color his female character with those feelings. His women might be stereotyped or merely shallow because of his avoidance. A male writer who holds women on a slightly elevated pedestal of esteem will possibly endow the female character with a coating of unearned sweetness or perfection or patience. A female writer, along the same lines, might, because of projected desires or subconscious fantasies, create supermen, or reduce male characters to unrealistic, incompetent wimps.

So the challenge presents itself. Regardless of what joys or atrocities a writer subjects his characters to, regardless of the strengths or weaknesses the writer bestows upon them, a writer must treat the characters fairly, in the sense that the characters are true to themselves, and not prodded along by a writer's misguided whims. In treating characters fairly, the writer does not betray the reader.

Horror fiction has traditionally put more females in perilous roles than it has males. And the females have fared worse for it. This, of course, could be based on the fact that horror tends to gravitate to the fantastic, and fantasy has usually, until quite recently, presented helpless females rescued by heroic males. Tradition changes slowly, as do attitudes and beliefs. The women's movement has affected all people, from the butcher to the baker to the horror novelist. Sensitivity heightened, sense of equality fine-tuned, horror writers are beginning to bring female characters into their own.

Does Dean Koontz do justice to his female characters?

* * * * * * *

Rebecca Chandler of *Darkfall* is a strong, single homicide detective who can hold her own with the best of her co-workers. She questions suspects cooly and efficiently; she views horribly disfigured corpses with the eye of an interested but detached examiner. Her personality is contrasted with that of her partner, Jack Dawson, father of two, who is unable or unwilling to be so distanced. As the story opens, Rebecca and Jack are investigating the body of a mutilated drug dealer. This death is one of the first hints that supernatural interferences are at work. Rebecca, who scoffs at Jack's beliefs in a possible link to the supernatural, seems relatively unaffected by the horrible scene.

> "These are rat bites," she said, "and they've disguised the real wounds. We'll have to wait for the autopsy to learn the cause of death...." Queasy, Jack turned away from the dead man. Rebecca continued to look. (1:23)

At the beginning, Koontz introduces Rebecca with all her stoicism and occupational drive. And yet, the reader is immediately thrown a curve, perhaps to soften the opinion of this tough woman, perhaps to mystify the reader as Jack is subsequently mystified. The reader is not shown whether Rebecca's speech is meant facetiously or with a bit of true longing.

> She stopped in the doorway and shook her head. "You know what I wish sometimes?" He stared at her. She said, "Sometimes I wish I'd married Tiny Taylor. Right now, I'd be up there in Connecticut, snug in my all-electric kitchen, having coffee and

> Danish, the kids off to school for the day, the twice-a-
> week maid taking care of the housework, looking
> forward to lunch at the country club with the girls..."
>   "Why is she doing this to me?" he wondered.
>   She noticed that he was still half out of his coat,
> and she said, "Didn't you hear me, Jack? We've got a
> call to answer."
>   "Yeah. I—"
>   "We've got two more stiffs" (1:18).

The police officers in Rebecca's department are uncomfortable with her presence. Concerning the first investigation, an officer corrects himself in front of her.

> The officer said, "See, this Parker broad...uh, I
> mean, this Miss Parker..."

When alone, however, the male officers are not quite so charitable.

> "I don't see how you put up with her, Jack....
> She's a regular cold one.... A real ball-buster!...a
> ball-*crusher*.... *Does* she go in for whips and
> chains.... Does she wear leather bras?"

And the infamous: "You're pussy-whipped, Jack" (1:33-34). This tirade is very probably true-to-life, but it is difficult to know whether or not it is solely critical or at all light-hearted. The reader has a difficult time interpreting the discussion, until the end of the section, where one is told that it is merely "good-natured abuse" (1:34), and Jack rides it out easily. Jack, it seems, is infatuated with his attractive partner.

The reader discovers that Rebecca is not a passive victim of her coworker's resentment. She retaliates with coarse, yet refreshing, banter.

> "He's extraordinarily tense this morning," Blaine
> said. "Extraordinarily tense."
>   "From the way he's acting," Rebecca said, "I
> thought maybe it was his time of the month" (1:29).

Although a cop with much experience and time in his profession, Jack still retains a romanticism, a chivalric if not sometimes moralistic view of women. His mental image of Rebecca is appealing, not gushy, making it easy for both male and female readers to appreciate her physical attributes.

Rebecca Chandler got out of the driver's side and slammed the door. Her long blond hair streamed behind her in the wind...Viking woman, Jack thought. Stoical. Resolute. And just look at that profile!

Her's was the noble, classic, feminine face that seafarers had once carved on the prows of their ships, ages ago, when such beauty was thought to have sufficient power to ward off the evils of the sea and the more vicious whims of fate (1:19).

When comparing Rebecca to a street-wise Shelly Parker, criminal Vince Vastagliano's girlfriend, Koontz moralizes a bit through Jack's eyes, discussing the qualities of women that men lust after and fantasize about as opposed to those men lust after, fantasize about, and marry. It distances the reader somewhat, not because of Jack's feelings, as these are true to his character, but because of the amount of space given these comparison thoughts. The space could cause a reader to feel Koontz is speaking here, not merely Jack musing (1:47-48).

As the challenges in *Darkfall* escalate, Rebecca's humaness, her softer side, comes through. She is forced to become a true partner to Jack within the realms of their work and private lives. Happily, she never evolves—or regresses—to the *hausfrau* to which she alluded at the opening of the novel. Her evolution is of a stronger kind, rounding out her character so she can embrace tenderness while retaining her personal inner strength. As terror mounts, evil forces gain in power, and Rebecca gives herself slowly but completely to Jack.

In *Darkfall*, sex embodies a power of its own, both for good and the evil. In the first of Jack's and Rebecca's successful physical encounters, Jack probes gently and persistently, drawing Rebecca out of her shell of caution. Rebecca, in relinquishing some of her reticence, acquires a new strength, and acknowledges her vulnerability.

"It hurt me, the way you were today," he said. "I thought you were disgusted with me, with yourself, for what we'd done."

"No. Never."

"I know that now, but here you are drawing away again, keeping me at arm's length. What's *wrong*?"

She chewed on·her thumb. Like a little girl.

"Rebecca?"

"I don't know how to say it. I don't know how to explain. I've never had to put it into words for anyone before." (1:158-59)

But she goes on to tell of her childhood, and the horrible experience of seeing her father blown to bits in the family sandwich shop, and then having the same happen to her mother not much later. Jack, surprised and sympathetic, is patient and supportive. The two form a bond not only of partners, but of lovers in the truest sense. Sex has provided a vehicle of cleansing and awakening.

On the other hand, sex is linked vitally with the power of evil, though not in such a detailed way. Koontz has created in Baba Lavelle a character of purest evil: a spiritual, sensual, base individual who exploits and harnesses all human desires, drives, and emotions. In an attempt to stop Jack from endangering Lavelle's pursuits, Lavelle decides to murder Jack's children.

> He didn't mind killing children. He looked forward to it. There was a special exhilaration in the murder of the very young. He licked his lips...Lavelle stripped out of his clothes. Fondling his genitals, he recited a short prayer. (1:121)

Linking sex, murder, and children seals Lavelle as one of the most frightening, detestable individuals in recent horror fiction.

As the tale reaches its climax, the bond formed by Rebecca and Jack is beautifully illustrated. Separated from each other for the entirety of the final conflict, each character must draw on what is his own and what each is to the other in order to defeat Lavelle and his hoards of seemingly indestructible demons. Love, openness, and trust have made Rebecca and Jack equals; Koontz has led them to become victors together.

> The wind was barely blowing now, but to his surprise it brought a voice to him. Rebecca's voice. Unmistakable. And four words that he much wanted to hear: "I love you, Jack."
> He turned, bewildered.
> She was nowhere in sight, yet her voice seemed to have been at his ear.
> He said, "I love you, too," and he knew that, wherever she was, she had heard him as clearly as he had heard her (1:280).

In contrast to Rebecca Chandler, Mary Bergen in *The Vision* is a dependent woman who openly admits her need for and her reliance on her husband, Max. As the story unfolds, it is clearly shown that except for her ability as a psychic, she has little confidence in herself. She suffers to share her talents with investigating officers; she gives herself to the point of exhaustion to save intended victims from a killer's grasp.

> ...she slumped against the door. She took several
> deep breaths. She was forced to relax periodically to
> regroup her energies if she were to maintain the psy-
> chic thread. For some clairvoyants, Barnes knew, the
> visions came without strain, virtually without effort;
> but apparently not for this one. (2:13)

But in spite of her self-sacrifice and insecurities, the reader, from the
beginning, is not presented with a stereotypical "weak" horror female
character. The entire first chapter, as a matter of fact, consists solely of
a journey with Mary through a clairvoyant excursion to thwart a murder. The reader is also given a large, impressive dose of Mary's inner
strength in the following chapters, being shown her deep dependence on
Max. Koontz has established her as sympathetic, not pathetic.

Characters in *The Vision* find Mary difficult to understand.
The police officers with whom she works regard her abilities as unusual, if not unnerving. Mary's psychiatrist, Dr. Cauvel, is fascinated
with her perceptions. He tests her twice a week in exchange for free
counseling, but the depths of her insight amaze and frighten him. Lou
Pasternak, a family friend and a "student of the occult," is an open-
minded individual who cannot have any true insight into what powers
are coming to the front, as Mary is unwittingly driven into the psychic
path of a new, unknown, and very brutal murderer. Likewise Max,
Mary's closest friend and lover, is very supportive yet is also confused
and alarmed.

The reader is not given a paragraph-long description of Mary's
physical features. Rather, she is described in smaller clips, much in the
way her thought processses are presented in bits and pieces.

> The perspiration of Mary Bergen's face was like
> the ceramic glaze on the plaster countenance of an al-
> tar saint. Her smooth skin gleamed in the green light
> from the instrument panel. Her dark eyes also shone,
> but they were unfocused (2:10).

And later:

> This woman was so lovely, charming, earnest, so
> convincing that perhaps she'd made a believer of him
> (2:12).

Still later, Mary is focused more by comparing and contrasting her with
her brother, Alan, and with Max.

> [Alan] had black hair and blue eyes, like Mary. He
> was handsome, while Max was so rough-hewn that he
> barely avoided ugliness (2:26).

In downplaying the details of his beautiful heroine, Koontz has made
her more universal in appeal.
    Similar to the way in which Shelly Parker is depicted in *Dark-
fall*, Miss Harrington, a minor female character in *The Vision*, is described in detail from a male's point of view. Her features, as shown,
seem to come more directly from Koontz than from the minds of the
police who have come to question her. She is not merely described, but
is evaluated.

> She was a petite blonde in her early forties. She
> had a lush figure, but she wasn't carrying any excess
> weight.
>   Apparently, her primary occupation was taking
> good care of herself.... (2:17).

The reader does not spend enough time with Miss Harrington to find
out if she is much more than a picturesque creature with orange finger-
nails and taut body.
    Mary, perhaps more so than other female protagonists in
Koontz novels, grows as the story progresses. At the onset, she depends on Max for everything, from being her "hand-holder" during
clairvoyant experiences to managing all of the couple's money. In
contradiction to his actual character, Alan correctly deduces Mary's true
relationship to Cauvel when he says,

> "You didn't marry him because he was exciting,
> or because he was intelligent or mysterious or roman-
> tic. You married him because he was big, strong, and
> gruff. A perfect father image" (2:32).

Mary relies on Dr. Cauvel to help her keep her balance:

> "I'll always need your help" (2:74).

But psychiatry loses its credibility and Max's strength seems faint.
When poltergeist-like occurrences drive Mary to believe that a spirit is
at work against her, she is no longer merely a sensitive psychic recipient. Glass figurines attack her in Dr. Cauvel's office, coming to life
only after Mary is near to seeing the face of the murderer. Mary is
awakened from a dream of the killer when a pistol, floating freely in
her bedroom, fires bullets toward the bed. Mary clings to Max, but it

is as though fate is shaking her from his arms, throwing her into a pit from which she alone must save herself.

Sex between Mary and Max is scant yet timely. Max is the giver, Mary the receiver. And yet, with Mary's situation and insecurities, this is as it should be, and gives the reader a few moments of comfort. When it is discovered by Mary and the reader simultaneously what "wicka wicka wicka" means, and why Mary has been haunted by other past sensations that are not, as she imagines, due to seeing her father die, the reader may well wonder if Mary might need to return to Cauvel for extensive therapy if she is ever to enjoy normal sex with Max again.

Surprisingly, Mary remains a frightened, somewhat impotent actor until a mere six pages from the end of the novel. It is as though she has grovels at the bottom of the pit, watching as flashes of light spark within her reach and then fade. Finally, the lights converge into a beam, that beam being clear memory of the day in the Mitchell's cabin when she was six *years* old, and only then is she able to leap upward and free herself with the power of anger and hatred. She has been horrendously raped, debased as much as any woman can be, and yet she becomes, momentarily, Anyman-Anywoman, who has the inner force of dignity and justice:

> She snapped. Abruptly, violently, her fear vanished.... She despised him. Loathed him. All she wanted was a chance to hurt him...to get him down, tie him down, torture him, cut him, choke him... (2:217).

Her revenge is just and profound.

The epilogue promises a brighter future. Knowing Mary as the reader has come to, there is hope that this is a true promise. Mary is strong now. She is no longer "afraid of the dark" (2:224). She is now in charge of herself and her destiny. Max seems grateful for the change. Hopefully, he will be able to adjust to her extensive growth.

* * * * * * *

Whispers presents an independent character by the name of Hilary Thomas. She is a single woman, a successful screenwriter who has moved from Chicago to a lovely mansion in Los Angeles. Unlike some other female protagonist counterparts, Hilary is a strong yet modest individual from the beginning of the tale. In spite of the fact that something from her past keeps her hesitant about forming relationships with others, men in particular, she is still a person of hope and faith, letting go of caution a little at a time to reap the benefits of a full life. Her creative sense of hope is obvious.

> And now I'm living in that dream, she thought.
> That make-believe place is real, and I own it.
> Maintaining the roses and the other plants...was
> not a chore. It was a joy. Every minute she worked
> among the flowers she was aware of how far she'd
> come (3:11).

But then an insane man breaks into her home in an attempt to rape and murder her. Hilary's cool head allows her to thwart his attempt, but after reporting the attack to the police, she is attacked in her home a second time. Her assailant, Bruno Frye, is determined to finish the job he had started. Hilary stops Frye again, killing him with a hidden knife. Hilary feels horrified by what has happened. She feels betrayed as well:

> ...Bruno Frye had taken that fragile dream by the
> throat and throttled it...[he] sent her tumbling back
> where she came from, down into doubt and fear and
> suspicion, down into the awful safety of loneliness
> (3:40-41).

Tony Clemenza, one of the two police officers who takes Hilary's report, becomes interested in her immediately. He must endure the brazenly critical assumptions of his partner Frank, who trusts no woman since his wife stole his money and left him. But Tony believes Hilary, and Hilary, in spite of having been so badly shaken, agrees to go out with him. Obviously, Hilary is stronger than she realized, and the reader feels comfortable with that strength. It allows the story to take off flying. It allows the tale to spend the majority of its energy with the character of Bruno Frye, which it is well advised to do. Having seen Hilary in action against Frye, the reader can know that, regardless of peril, Hilary will put up the good fight.

The description of Hilary, given through Tony's eyes, might well be a distraction from her other qualities. Not that beauty and brains can't exist simultaneously, and work well together, but a particular description may tint a reader's feelings toward Hilary. After seeing how beautiful she is, from her flawless complexion to the "perfect shape of her patrician nose" to her enormous eyes and thick raven hair, the reader is told that her face is balanced by "the almost obscene fullness of her lips." (3:68) Female readers could easily be put off by this description. It seems sluttish. Male readers might be intrigued by the same sluttish connotations. Either way, it is a small statement with the ability to snag the reader. Hilary has to prove herself beyond this.

Lana Haverby is the minor female character that is, as happens in *Darkfall* and *The Vision*, used as a comparison, both mentally and physically, to Hilary Thomas. Tony is more of a moralizer than Jack

Dawson. Interspersed with dialogue concerning a convict Tony is seeking, the description of Lana consists of three paragraphs. Again, statements or evaluations made here don't seem to do anything for the story line.

> Her legs were okay, but the rest of her was far from prime.... Her gelatinous breast jiggled and swayed alarmingly, in what she evidently thought was a wildly provocative display. She affected that ass-swinging, tippy-toe-walk that didn't look good on any coquette over twenty-one; she was forty, a grown woman unable to discover and explore the dignity and special beauty of her own age, trying to pass for a teenager, and she was pathetic (3:127-129).

Granted, a woman of Lana's type is certainly realistic. But the amount of space given Tony's observation, and the evaluation of her, makes a look at Lana seem like a mini-sermon. The reader might want to determine for himself/herself if Lana is pathetic.

Except for Hilary's repeated resistance to admit her love for Tony, there is an equalness between these two major characters. Their first date is exemplary, full of humorous, lively bantering as the two size each other up:

> "I've already lost my head over you," [said Tony].
> Hilary groaned.
> "Too saccharine?" he asked.
> "I need a bit of lemon after that one."
> "But you liked it."
> "Yes, I admit I did. I guess I'm a sucker for flattery." (3:179-80)

After this first date Hilary, alone in her house, can't get Tony out of her mind:

> Half an hour later, upstairs, in bed, Hilary's body ached with frustration. Her breasts were full and taut; she longed to feel his hands on them.... She tossed and turned for maybe an hour before she finally got up and took a sedative (3:198).

Another woman in Hilary's position would have most likely masturbated, hopefully to climax, or if not, at least with fingers pretending to be her lover, dreaming, wishing. Hilary, as independent as she is, seems like the type of woman who would have no problem with this. It could have been described without resorting to graphics. Would she have been too much like Lana with this approach to horniness? Would Tony-Koontz feel that this would make her less than perfect if she so indulged?

When Tony and Hilary finally consumate their relationship, and the experience continues for nearly four pages, the effect on the reader is sensuously staggering. The mutual respect along with the erotic quality of the prose creates a scene not soon forgotten, particularly when Tony discovers a cruel scar along Hilary's side, traveling from her belly to back. He sees it not as distracting or ugly, but as something that emphasizes her beauty even more. He knows that she has, in some way, suffered painfully. He does not pity her, but is increasingly respectful. Hilary is embarrassed, but says nothing.

The bond between Tony and Hilary strengthens as the two, together, seek out the unexplained "revival" of Bruno Frye. Bruno, who apparently has come to life again, believes that his abusive, deceased mother is being repeatedly reincarnated as different women, and he must kill these women to save himself. The remainder of the novel consists of unraveling the mystery. Intermissions of uninhibited, enjoyable sex give brief respites from the horror. Hilary and Tony work now as a balanced unit; Hilary's courage and ability, shown to the reader at the very beginning of the story, do not falter. The reader can count on Hilary and can therefore more completely become carried away with the evil, fascinating works of Bruno Frye.

Two female characters share the limelight in *Night Chills*. Jenny Edison is a young, attractive woman who lives with her father and is a partner with him, running Edison's General Store in Black River, Maine. She has discovered that Black River is the haven she needs, a soul-soothing asylum from California and a soured, seven-year marriage to a self-centered musician. A year earlier, she met Paul Annendale, a widower, who vacations in the small town, bringing his two children to the country for hiking and camping. Jenny and her father are well-respected members of the Black River community. Before actually "meeting" Jenny, the reader is introduced to her through the memories and anticipations of Paul:

> Paul had met Jenny Edison just last year...catching sight of her, Paul had for a moment been unable to get his breath.
>
> It happened that quickly between them. Not love at first sight. Something more fundamental than love. Something more basic that had to come first, before love could develop.... Jenny felt the attraction too, powerfully, immediately—but almost unwillingly (4:43-44).

The "something special" isn't strong enough to allow Jenny to trust romance again.

Rya Annendale, age eleven, is undoubtedly a precocious, worthy character. She is bright, observant, and sensitive. She has had a happy childhood, shadowed by the death of her mother, but enlightened by the love and support of her father. Rya does more than tolerate her younger brother; she reacts with mature concern when he is unhappy. She does more than watch the relationship between her father and Jenny, she encourages it. The reader is given a hopeful feeling that Rya will prove to be more than an average, minor, child character. Luckily, that hope is not left unsated.

Physically, Jenny is a beautiful, slender, dark-haired woman. She is described through the mental scrutiny of Paul as he rides with her to a tavern for their first date of the season:

> Her face—too beautiful to appear in *Vogue*: she
> would have made the other models in the magazine
> look like horses—was in repose. Her full lips were
> slightly parted as she sang softly with the music and
> this bit of animation, this parting of the lips had more
> sensual impact than a heavy-eyed, full-faced leer from
> Elizabeth Taylor (4:45).

Unlike the female protagonists in *Darkfall* and *Whispers*, Jenny is not morally judged or substantiated through the eyes of a man. And opposed to *Darkfall*, *The Vision*, and *Whispers*, Jenny is not contrasted by a male protagonist to a sexually blatant beauty of, as is hinted, less character. This is to Jenny's advantage. One female comes close, the waitress Alice, to whom evil Ogden Salsbury compares his wife in the early years. But a comparison by Odgen doesn't affect the reader very much, as it is not he with whom the reader would likely identify. Therefore, the reader can be the judge of Alice, and more importantly, of Jenny.

Rya, pictured lovingly through the eyes of her father, is slim, blue-eyed, with long brown hair. And as a father would describe through the pride of parenthood, Rya is shown not so much physically as through her characterization, her appealing traits, her peculiar and lovable habits.

Jenny resists a serious relationship with the persistent Paul at first, but she admits she loves him. It is marriage she fears. However, in terms of sexual interest and drive, she is Paul's equal. Jenny can become sexually involved quickly, she can initiate it, and can joke about sex easily:

> Suddenly she became the bolder of the two. She
> rubbed one hand across the crotch of his jeans, felt
> him swelling beneath the denim.
> "I want that," she said. "...I can't help it if I'm
> horny."
> "You're more than horny."
> "Oversexed, then."
> "It's not just sex," he said.
> "You're not going to tell me you like my mind,
> too."
> "...You've got a lust for life."
> "Me and Van Gogh." (4:109-110)

Sex between Jenny and Paul exemplifies their affection for each other, but it clarifies Jenny's reluctance to commit herself to marriage's legalities. This reluctance remains throughout the novel, until crisis opens her eyes to life beyond the original pain of failed love.

The evil that confronts Jenny, Rya, Paul, and the residents of Black River originates in the brilliant, warped mind of scientist Ogden Salsbury. Ogden has developed a drug that makes people receptive, unconditionally so, to subliminal control. Although a near genius, Ogden is an individual with twisted intentions, rooted in a nightmarish childhood. The nightmare consisted of the women in Ogden's life. His mother beat him mercilessly. His mother's lover raped him when he was eleven while his mother stood by and watched. Ogden was put into a foster home with all girls. According to Ogden's foster father, Mr. Barger,

> "The older girls knew what had happened to him.
> They used to tease him something fierce. He couldn't
> take it. He'd blow up everytime...Of course that was
> what they wanted, so they just teased him some
> more."

Mr. Barger, a stereotypical male chauvinist, in trying to help Ogden deal with his dilemma, sealed in Ogden's soul a most hideous attitude concerning woman:

> Mr. Barger said, "I'd take him aside and talk to
> him—almost father to son. I used to tell him not to
> pay them any mind. I used to tell him that they were
> just women and that women were good for only two
> things. Fucking and cooking" (4:207).

The impact of this on the reader is as sickening as Ogden's rape. Ogden's unbalanced psyche is irreparably damaged by ignorance.

Ogden sees his subliminal control as a means of regaining power he never had as a child or even as an adult. And, of course, much of the power he seeks consists of having women debase themselves for his sexual and temporary emotional gratification.

Rya is the first to witness the horrors of Ogden's subliminal powers. Bob Thorp, police chief and friend of the Edisons, kills Rya's brother Mark as Rya, at first undetected, watches from outside. Rya fights the disbelief of her father and Jenny, holding to her story regardless of the terror. Her bravery allows her to break back into the Thorp home to find proof of the murder—a bucket of bloody rags hidden beneath the sink.

Both Jenny's and Rya's characters are changed, are deepened, through the course of the tale. Although the two of them fade from the forefront a bit as the conflict begins to escalate, they are pivotal in the climax. Jenny and Rya, hiding in a belltower, try to keep safe as Paul and Sam Edison face off Ogden Salsbury and his mind-controlled troops, but are confronted by a partner of Ogden's, Ernst Klinger. With enviable courage, they stage their own turntable surprise attack, killing Klinger.

Fighting with Paul has eased Jenny's marital fears. Together, they launch a new future with Rya's blessings. Rya, although still somewhat stunned by all the terrors she has faced, is able to look ahead with hope. At the conclusion of the novel, the reader might begin to wonder what kind of adult heroine Rya would make. It is interesting to ponder, considering the strength already such an integral part of her.

* * * * * * *

Does Dean Koontz do justice to his female characters?

The females in *Darkfall*, *The Vision*, *Whispers*, and *Night Chills* are strong individuals in their own right. All different on certain levels, they are all masters of their own fates. They are intelligent characters. They are sexual equals to their partners. Although they are sometimes judged, fairly or not so fairly, by their male counterparts, they shine through, allowing the reader, after working through the perils with them, to make his/her own judgment calls.

It would be a curious thing to see Koontz write of a not-so-beautiful heroine; to have her as interesting and strong as his gorgeous protagonists. The fantasy aspect of horror need not always play on fantasy wishes. The male protagonists are not always attractive—Max, of *The Vision*, is a wonderful, appealing individual who is described as being very close to ugly.

Dean Koontz treats his female characters, and his male characters, fairly. They are true to themselves. Male or female, their actions reveal a writer who does not guide his characters but follows their lead.

166

The reader of Koontz novels is not betrayed. On the contrary. The reader is delighted.

XII.

AFTERWORD

BY JOE R. LANSDALE

Dean Koontz is one of our great storytellers. Right in there with such contemporary masters as John D. MacDonald, Stephen King, and a drunk I used to know who was never published but told some real whoppers when he was in a pickled condition.

Other than being a great storyteller, Dean is also a great phone conversationalist and is responsible for a large portion of my long-distance telephone bill. Whenever I call Dean or I get a call from him, I usually lie down on the bed and hook up the intravenous feeding, because I know I'm going to be a while. Of course, to hear Dean tell it, I'm the one that does all the talking, the one that just won't shut up, but hey, we know who to believe, don't we?

The problem is, over the phone or in person, Dean is just as fascinating as his books. He also has pretty good color coordination with his clothes and he can ballroom dance, as he and his lovely wife Gerda have been practicing this for some time now. So, if the conversation lags, Dean can always break into a fox trot, though over the phone this isn't nearly as entertaining as it might be in person. Still, you can hear the music and the precise shuffle of Dean's feet as he goes through his paces in two/four time.

Now wait a minute. I just lied. Not about the fox trot—well, maybe I lied a little. But what I really told a windy about is Dean being as interesting as his books. Dean is interesting, but the truth is, nothing he's ever said has matched the excitement of *Watchers* or the mystery and humanity of *Strangers*, the pure unsettling terror of *Whispers*, *Face of Fear*, or *Shattered*. And better yet, the books are entertaining without just being entertainments of the sort you can read while glancing at an episode of *Three's Company* in rerun or listening to the latest Heavy Metal hit on full volume.

Sure, his books are fun. I'm not trying to imply that they are stuffy, or that the prose makes you work as hard as a one-legged field hand just to understand what is being said. Far from it. Dean's prose is crisp as fresh lettuce and clear as the moon on a hot Texas night. Still, more goes on in a Koontz scene than just the scene. The pages

168

are more than a specialized wood product with printed matter on them. They have an echo that reverberates long after the book has been put down. And that, friends and neighbors, is what real writing is all about.

Echo.

Few writers have it. Many put one word after another well enough, like placing dead beetles in a row, but those beetles, being dead, will never beat their wings, click their mandibles, or twitch their legs. Dead prose, like a dead bug, is simply dead.

A page of Koontz, on the other hand, is brilliantly alive. His words are not dead beetles. They are more akin to brightly-colored honey bees, busy and full of purpose. They are pure examples of the storyteller's art. Like the works of Dickens, Kipling, London, Twain, MacDonald, or King, they are alive and they are for everyone. Rich or poor. The average reader, the scholarly reader. Dean's books embrace you and they kick your ass. They show you light and they show you shadow. They are the truth, dear hearts, no matter what guise the stories take. And the truth has echo.

It's good to have a writer like Dean Koontz. His works are a treasure to us all.

So Dean, stay at it. But next time you call, don't call collect for Christsakes, and turn off that damn fox trot music and put on something sensible like Hank Williams or Loretta Lynn. And most important, write on, friend. Write on. You are an example to us all, and we eagerly await your next creation.

—Joe R. Lansdale
Nacogdoches, Texas

ABOUT THE CONTRIBUTORS

STAN BROOKS is a Graduate of the University of the State of New York and holds a B.S. in Liberal Arts. He is a 1st Lieut. in the USAF reserves, and works as a physician's assistant in the Otolaryngology Department in Basset Hospital, Cooperstown, New York. His fiction has appeared in *Footsteps #VII*. Stan is married and has two children.

MICHAEL R. COLLINGS is a Professor of English at Pepperdine University. His publications include: *The Films of Stephen King, Brian Aldiss, Naked to the Sun: Dark Visions of Apocalypse, The Many Facets of Stephen King, Stephen King as Richard Bachman, Scaring Us to Death, The Work of Stephen King*, and many more. He lives with his wife and four children in Southern California.

JOE R. LANSDALE lives in Texas with his wife Karen and their two children. Joe's entrance to writing included such colorful jobs as a bouncer, a bodyguard, a martial arts instructor, a rose field worker, and a farmer. His fiction includes *Dead in the West* (Space and Time), *The Magic Wagon* (Doubleday), *Act of Love* (Zebra), *The Nightrunners* (Dark Harvest), and *The Drive-In* (Doubleday). His interviews with Dean Koontz, Robert R. McCammon, and J. K. Potter have appeared in *Twilight Zone Magazine*. His short story, "Tight Little Stitches in a Dead Man's Back," has been chosen to appear in Karl Edward Wagner's *Year's Best Horror*.

RICHARD LAYMON, a resident of California, is a well-published author. His works include *Tread Softly* (Tor), *Night Show* (Tor), *The Cellar* (Warner), *Out Are the Lights* (Warner), and *The Woods Are Dark* (Warner). He was a school librarian at one time and is now a part-time writer.

ELIZABETH MASSIE, a graduate of James Madison University in Harrisonburg, VA, is an elementary teacher in Hugh Cassell Elementary School in Augusta County, VA. Her fiction has appeared in *The Horror Show, Footsteps*, and *Grue*. Her short story, "Hooked on Buzzer," has been published in *Women of Darkness* (Tor). She is married and has two children.

MICHAEL MORRISON, a professor at the University of Oklahoma, has a Ph.D. in Physics. In addition to writing book reviews for *Fantasy Review*, he is currently working on *After the Danse: Horror Fiction in the Eighties*. In addition, his textbook, *The Joy of Quantum Physics*, was published by Prentice-Hall in 1988.

BILL MUNSTER lives in Round Top, New York, where he teaches English at a local academy. He also edits the acclaimed magazine of dark fantasy, *Footsteps*.

TIM POWERS is a full-time writer. He graduated from California State University, Fullerton with a B.A. in English. Tim's novels include *Dinner at Deviant's Palace, The Anubis Gates, The Stress of Her Regard, On Stranger Tides*, and *The Drawing of the Dark*. He is also the recipient of the Philip K. Dick Award for his fiction. He currently lives in Southern California.

DAVID TAYLOR, a professor at Moravian College in Bethlehem, PA, earned a B.A. from the University of Tennessee, an M.A. from Arkansas State, and a D.A. from the University of Mississippi. He teaches expository writing and creative writing, and is the director of English tutorship. His first professional short story recently appeared in *Footsteps* #VIII.

ACKNOWLEDGMENTS

"A Dean Koontz Interview," by Bill Munster. Portions of this interview were previously published in *Night Cry*, and in *Footsteps* #VI.

"Dean Koontz and Stephen King: Style, *Invasion*, and an Aesthetics of Horror," by Michael R. Collings. Substantially different versions of this article were published as Chapter VIII, "Speculations," in *Stephen King as Richard Bachman*, and as "King Versus Koontz: Style and Invasions" in *Footsteps* #VIII (November, 1986), edited by Bill Munster.

NOTES

CHAPTER X

[1]Letter, January 31, 1986. In spite of fragments of poetry published as epigrams and attributed to the *Book of Sorrows*, Koontz has published no collection of poetry, even though *Contemporary Authors* identifies *The Time the Place* (Advent, 1969) as poetry. He does, however, have an interest in poetry, as his work in *Twilight Eyes* demonstrates.

[2]Berkley published *Twilight Eyes* in a paperback edition; the book does not include the illustrations, but does contain a brief sequel. To that extent, to appreciate *Twilight Eyes* fully will require readers to work with both texts, since the Land of Enchantment edition has a shorter text, while the Berkley edition foregoes the power of the limited edition's artwork and production values.

WORKS CITED

NOTE: Only those chapters where works are cited by number are included in this listing. For all other citations, the reader should refer to the bibliography.

CHAPTER VI

1. *Soft Come the Dragons*, by Dean Koontz. New York: Ace Books, 1970.
2. *How To Write Best-Selling Fiction*, by Dean Koontz. Cincinnati, OH: Writer's Digest Books, 1981.
3. Dean Koontz interview with Stan Brooks, January 27, 1987.
4. *The Flesh in the Furnace*, by Dean Koontz. New York: Bantam Books, 1973.
5. *A Darkness in My Soul*, by Dean Koontz. New York: DAW Books, 1970.
6. *The Eyes of Darkness*, by Dean Koontz. New York: Pocket Books, 1981.
7. *Darkfall*, by Dean Koontz. New York: Berkley Books, 1984.

CHAPTER VII

1. *Eichmann in Jerusalem: A Study in the Banality of Evil*, by Hannah Arendt. New York: Harcourt, Brace, 1963.
2. *Phantoms*, by Dean Koontz. New York: Berkley Books, 1983. Subsequent references are to this edition and are noted parenthetically by page.
3. *Strangers*, by Dean Koontz. New York: Berkley Books, 1986. Subsequent references are to this edition and are noted parenthetically by page.
4. *Whispers*, by Dean Koontz. New York: Berkley Books, 1981. Subsequent references are to this edition and are noted parenthetically by page.
5. "Dean of Suspense: An Interview with Dean R. Koontz," by Joe R. Lansdale. *Twilight Zone Magazine* (December, 1986): 22-24.

CHAPTER VIII

1. Interview with Dean Koontz by Ed Gorman, in *Mystery Scene Reader* (1987).
2. *Watchers*, by Dean Koontz. New York: G. P. Putnam's Sons, 1987.
3. *Frankenstein*, by Mary Wollstonecraft Shelley. New York: Bantam Pathfinder Editions, 1967.
4. *Shadowfires*, by Dean Koontz as "Leigh Nichols." New York: Avon Books, 1987.
5. Interview with Dean Koontz by Stan Brooks, March 1987.

CHAPTER IX

1. *Phantoms,* by Dean Koontz. New York: G. P. Putnam's Sons, 1986.
2. *Whispers,* by Dean Koontz. New York: G. P. Putnam's Sons, 1980; New York: Berkley Books, 1981.
3. *Darkfall,* by Dean Koontz. New York: Berkley Books, 1984; London: W. H. Allen, 1984.

CHAPTER XI

1. *Darkfall,* by Dean Koontz. London: W. H. Allen, 1984.
2. *The Vision,* by Dean Koontz. New York: G. P. Putnam's Sons, 1977.
3. *Whispers,* by Dean Koontz. New York: G. P. Putnam's Sons, 1980.
4. *Night Chills,* by Dean Koontz. New York: Atheneum, 1976.

BIBLIOGRAPHY

Arendt, Hannah. *Eichmann in Jerusalem: A Study in the Banality of Evil.* New York: Harcourt, Brace, 1963.

Collings, Michael R. *Stephen King as Richard Bachman.* Mercer Island, WA: Starmont House, 1985.

Collings, Michael R., and David A. Engebretson. *The Shorter Works of Stephen King.* Mercer Island, WA: Starmont House, 1985.

Gorman, Ed. "Interview," in *Mystery Scene.*

Grabowski, William. "Interview with Dean R. Koontz," in *The Horror Show* (Summer 1986).

King, Stephen. *The Bachman Books.* New York: NAL, 1985.

King, Stephen. *Carrie.* Garden City, NY: Doubleday, 1974.

King, Stephen. *Christine.* New York: Viking, 1983.

King, Stephen. *Cycle of the Werewolf.* New York: Signet, 1985.

King, Stephen. *The Dark Tower: The Gunslinger.* West Kingston, RI: Donald Grant, 1982.

King, Stephen. *The Eyes of the Dragon.* Bangor, ME: Philtrum Press, 1984.

King, Stephen. *IT.* New York: Viking, 1986.

King, Stephen. "On *The Shining* and Other Perpetrations," in *Whispers* #17/18 (August, 1982).

King, Stephen [as Richard Bachman]. *Rage.* New York: Signet, 1981.

King, Stephen [as Richard Bachman]. *The Running Man.* New York: Signet, 1982.

King, Stephen. *'Salem's Lot.* Garden City, NY: Doubleday, 1975.

King, Stephen. *The Shining.* Garden City, NY: Doubleday, 1977.

King, Stephen. *The Stand.* Garden City, NY: Doubleday, 1978.

King, Stephen [with Peter Straub]. *The Talisman.* New York: Viking, 1984.

King, Stephen [as Richard Bachman]. *Thinner.* New York: NAL, 1984.

Koontz, Dean. *After the Last Race.* New York: Atheneum, 1974.

Koontz, Dean. *Anti-Man.* New York: Paperback Library, 1970.

Koontz, Dean. *Darkfall.* New York: Berkley, 1984; W. H. Allen, 1984.

Koontz, Dean. *A Darkness in My Soul.* New York: Daw, 1970.

Koontz, Dean. *The Eyes of Darkness.* New York: Pocket, 1981.

Koontz, Dean. *The Face of Fear.* Indianapolis, IN: Bobbs-Merrill, 1977.

Koontz, Dean. *The Flesh in the Furnace* New York: Bantam, 1973.

Koontz, Dean. *How to Write Best Selling Horror Fiction.* Ohio: Writer's Digest Books, 1981.

Koontz, Dean [as Aaron Wolfe]. *Invasion.* Don Mills, Ontario: Laser Books, 1975.

Koontz, Dean. Letter to Michael R. Collings, January 14, 1986.

Koontz, Dean. Letter to Michael R. Collings, January 31, 1986.

Koontz, Dean. Letter to Stan Brooks, January 27, 1987.

Koontz, Dean. Letter to Stan Brooks, March, 1987.

Koontz, Dean. *Night Chills*. New York: Atheneum, 1976; New York: Berkley Books, 1983.

Koontz, Dean. *Nightmare Journey*. New York: Berkley, 1975.

Koontz, Dean. *Phantoms*. New York: G. P. Putnam's Sons, 1983.

Koontz, Dean [as Leigh Nichols]. *Shadowfires*. New York, Avon, 1987.

Koontz, Dean [as K. R. Dwyer]. *Shattered*. New York: Random House, 1973; as Koontz: New York: Berkley Books, 1985.

Koontz, Dean. *Soft Come the Dragons*. New York: Ace, 1970.

Koontz, Dean. *Strangers*. New York: G. P. Putnam's Sons, 1986.

Koontz, Dean. *Twilight Eyes*. Plymouth, MI: Land of Enchantment, 1985.

Koontz, Dean. *The Vision*. New York: G. P. Putnam's Sons, 1977.

Koontz, Dean. *The Voice of the Night*. Garden City, NY: Doubleday, 1980.

Koontz, Dean. *Warlock*. New York: Lancer, 1972.

Koontz, Dean. *Watchers*. New York: G. P. Putnam's Sons, 1987.

Koontz, Dean. *A Werewolf Among Us*. New York: Ballantine, 1973.

Koontz, Dean. *Whispers*. New York: G. P. Putnam's Sons, 1980; Berkley, 1981.

Landsdale, Joe R. "Dean of Suspense: An Interview with Dean Koontz," in *Twilight Zone Magazine* (December 1986).

Munster, Bill. "An Interview with Dean Koontz," in *Footsteps* #VI (1985).

Shelley, Mary. *Frankenstein*. New York: Bantam, 1967.

INDEX

www.ingramcontent.com/pod-product-compliance
Lightning Source LLC
Chambersburg PA
CBHW031259090426
42742CB00007B/523